Rock

Chalk!

Todd

#5

Rock Chuck!

Total #5

FOR Jayhawks Fans ONLY!

Wonderful Stories Celebrating the Incredible Fans of the Kansas Jayhawks

By Matt Fulks and Rich Wolfe

Foreword by Jayhawks Greats, Players, Coaches, and Fans

ASCEND BOOKS

www.ascendbooks.com

10 9 8 7 6 5 4 3 2 1

Printed in the United States of America

ISBN-13: 978-0-9817166-9-5
ISBN-10: 0-9817166-9-5

Library of Congress Cataloging-in-Publications Data Available Upon Request

Editor: Lee Stuart
Design: Randy Lackey, The Covington Group

This book is not an official publication of, nor is it endorsed by,
the University of Kansas.

www.ascendbooks.com

FOR Jayhawks Fans ONLY!

Wonderful Stories Celebrating the Incredible Fans of the Kansas Jayhawks

Special Thanks To:

Acknowledgments

A lot of people helped to bring this book to fruition. As always, I'll go ahead and say now that if I forget to mention you by name, still know that I am thinking about you ... just not as I write this.

To Whitney Barnes, Kerry Comiskey, Bob Snodgrass and the rest of the gang at Ascend Books for your assistance, guidance, and willingness to get this book on the shelves. A special thanks to editor Lee Stuart, who helped mold this and provided endless support and encouragement, while displaying the patience of a yeoman. To co-author Rich Wolfe, who came up with the idea of these fan books several years ago and realized there would be a great wealth of KU stories. To Leif Lisec and John Sprugel at Metro Sports for your assistance and support.

To my relatives, friends, former co-workers, Jayhawks in charge of watch parties, and Facebook fans of the book, who submitted stories, agreed to interviews, or at least passed along the word of this book to other Jayhawks. Word of this book spread across the country thanks to your help. Because of that, we received a lot of stories worthy of inclusion in the book, but we were unable to include everything received because of space. Guess we'll have to start planning Volume 2.

To my business partner and lifelong chum, Chris Garrett, who's a die-hard Jayhawk.

To my agent, Rob Wilson, who patiently put another project on hold while I wrote this book.

To the group of friends and family who serve as my core support, encouragement and guidance, I owe a mountain of gratitude: Tom Lawrence, Denny Matthews, Jim Wissel. Plus, Steve and Denise Treece, and Tim and Amy Brown — who are an endless source of encouragement. I'll never tell you how much your friendship means. I have to add that I prayed a lot during this project, particularly the last few weeks approaching (and passing) deadline. I felt like a slow, short guard trying to defend Calvin Thompson or Ron Kellogg. So, without Christ this isn't possible. Finally, special thanks to my favorite in-laws, Todd and Pat Burwell; and my parents, Fred and Sharon, who served as encouragers and babysitters. To my best friend, Libby, who kept her sanity when I lost mine; and our three children, Helen, Charlie, and Aaron, who made it through their summer vacation while I scrounged for stories. I guess they love me anyway.

Thank you, all.

Table of Contents

Foreword
A Collection of Favorite Memories from KU Fans

One of the greatest things about being associated with the University of Kansas for more than 60 years is the people. The people at the university and, of course, the wonderful fans. There were so many times during my career — and since — when fans made me feel really special.

Those kinds of things make an impression on you and make you realize that people appreciate the work I did for 60 years. That's a great feeling.

Max Falkenstien – Legendary Broadcaster

A little over 40 years ago, I lost what I thought was the toughest battle in sports, in losing to the North Carolina Tar Heels by one point in triple-overtime. It was a devastating thing for me because I felt as though I let the University of Kansas down and my teammates down. But now I realize that it was just a loss of a game by how many people have shown me so much appreciation and love and warmth from the University of Kansas. I'm a Jayhawk and I know why there's so much tradition here, and so many wonderful things have come from here, and I'm very much a part of it and very proud of it. Rock Chalk, Jayhawk!

Wilt Chamberlain – Basketball Hall of Famer

As an old guy who's been around Lawrence longer than I anticipated, having that appreciation for what our teams accomplished and now to enjoy it as a fan, is what living is all about. The fans are one reason that it's so great to continue living in Lawrence.

Bud Stallworth – KU Basketball Great

I can say, throughout my entire collegiate career, to even today, I can't walk inside Allen Fieldhouse without getting goosebumps. There's a tremendous awe and history every time I go in there. I have a feeling that as long as Bill Self is the basketball coach, those goosebumps will continue.

Steve Beaumont – Former KU Yell Leader

I'm living an out-of-body experience in my life and my career and the things I've been involved with. KU athletics is at the top of that list.

Miles Schnaer – KU Booster

Introduction

Rich Wolfe is crazy — this won't work!

At least that's what I thought when Wolfe, a friend and fellow author, called me in 2002 to tell me about a new series of books he was starting to compile, *For _____ Fans Only*. (Insert your favorite team.) The idea being that each book in the series would be a collection of fans telling their favorite, funniest, most poignant, most memorable stories about ... well, being fans.

As soon as I started helping compile some stories for one of the first books in the series, *For Cubs Fans Only*, I realized Rich was on to something. Fans did have stories to tell! Almost immediately, Rich and I started talking about teams in the Kansas City area that might have passionate enough fans with similarly good stories. That led us here.

Because of my appreciation for teams from the University of Kansas, Rich and I started talking about doing a *For Jayhawk Fans Only* book. For whatever reason, that Jayhawk didn't hatch. Until now.

I need to clarify the statement, "my appreciation for teams from the University of Kansas," however. Several years ago, I had an alum from another Big 12 school, who when realizing I pulled for the Jayhawks but didn't attend KU, said, "Oh, you're one of *those* fans." So, yes, I guess I'm one of *those* fans ... the person who grew up in the Kansas City area, pulling for KU — after moving here from Columbia, Missouri, mind you — who went to college in another state, and yet continued to follow his childhood team.

Today, with three KU books on the shelves, plus relationships I've developed at the University, I hope each Jayhawk team is successful for years to come. So, yes, there are some like me who didn't attend the university but still pull for its teams as hard as any alum.

That's the thing about Jayhawk Nation. It consists of fans of every type. Take Bob Davis, for example. The long-time "voice" of the Jayhawks is a graduate of Washburn University. You'll be able to read Bob's story in this book. For those of you in Kansas City, you might know that Mick Shaffer of Metro Sports is a die-hard Oklahoma State fan — and a KU grad. He doesn't have a story in the book, but one of his co-workers at Metro, Erik Ashel, does. Erik is a Jayhawk, through and through.

There is a story from a 13-year-old boy in Chicago who already has the date circled for when he can attend the University of Kansas. There are stories of Jayhawk fans who didn't see a game at Allen Fieldhouse or Memorial Stadium until late in life. And others who have early childhood memories of meeting guys like Max Falkenstien, Wilt Chamberlain, Jim Ryun, and Danny Manning. And Kansas City newscaster John Holt, who once had a run-in with an, um, older woman after a basketball game in Manhattan because he is a KU fan.

In much the same way you can't control fans during a game (or afterwards), there's no controlling fans in *For Jayhawk Fans Only*. As you know, your memories of your team — the Jayhawks, the Kansas City Royals, the Chicago Cubs, whatever team — can't be manufactured. You might not have a great story about KU winning the 1988 national title in basketball that you share with your buddies, but you might have a hilarious tale about sneaking into Allen Fieldhouse in 1977 that's become part of your personal Jayhawk lore. Same holds true for this book. This is not a history of the University of Kansas athletics. It doesn't mention each great coach or terrific player, or every championship team.

This is a collection of fans' memories. And, no, it's not a collection of former players and famous alums telling their favorite stories. The only former athletes featured here are Chuck Dobson, Steve Renko, Bud Stallworth, and Calvin Thompson. Chuck, Steve, and Calvin all grew up in the Kansas City area — not far from the KU campus, went to KU and remain passionate Jayhawk fans. Bud, who might be one of the biggest Jayhawk fans out there, has remained in Lawrence largely because of the KU fans.

And, although there might be some other recognizable names with feature stories in this book, *For Jayhawk Fans Only* is a collection of fans, just like you, who had favorite, funny, poignant, memorable stories to share. Hmmmm. Just like my co-author Rich Wolfe said they would.

Sorry, Rich, I was wrong. I've never been so wrong. Well, as I've written before, the only other time I was this wrong was when I thought painting my nails blue in 1997 in honor of Scot Pollard would be a cool good luck charm. Try explaining that one when you're wearing sandals in a Georgia convenience store. As it turned out, the Jayhawks lost to Arizona. At least I escaped the convenience store. Good luck for me; not so much for the Jayhawks.

Although we had to turn down some stories because of space limitations or because they came in after deadline (and we hope to include those in Volume 2), *For Jayhawk Fans Only* offers a wonderful collection of stories from some of the best fans in the country. And it reminds each fan — regardless of how you got here — why you love to chant: "Rock ... Chalk ... Jayhawk ... go KU!"

MWF
August 16, 2009 (aka "Elvis Day")

CHAPTER 1

I Saw It on the Radio

Max Falkenstien

During a 60-year career, spanning 1946-2006, Max Falkenstien announced 650 Jayhawk football games and 1,750 KU basketball games, including every men's basketball game played at Allen Fieldhouse from 1 955-2006. Falkenstien has been honored by the Naismith Basketball Hall of Fame, the College Football Hall of Fame, the KU Hall of Fame, and the state of Kansas Hall of Fame.

Max Falkenstien

Photo courtesy of Matt Fulks

One of the greatest things about being associated with the University of Kansas for more than 60 years is the people. The people at the university and, of course, the wonderful fans.

There were so many times during my career — and since — when fans made me feel really special. One time that stands out was when the K-Club named me an honorary letterman and gave me a mythical "K," symbolic of being a letterman. That was a nice gesture that I certainly was fond of at the time. All of the honors and Hall of Fame awards that I've received came later in my career. These days, wherever I go, it seems like people recognize me and say, "Hi, Max, we sure enjoyed listening to you and enjoyed what you did." I hear things like that on almost a daily basis. That's nice. People ask for autographs and pictures and that sort of thing. Dads, a lot of times, want to have me take a picture with their sons and daughters, which is nice. I doubt the kids appreciate it, but I think the dads do.

Fans have been as good in each era — before the giant video board and the Internet, and cable TV, even before all of the games were televised — as they are today. There was tremendous interest. Of course, we didn't have the television and other media coverage that's available today. The first TV broadcast of a KU game was called by Jay Barrington on WDAF in Kansas City. That was a big deal because no games prior to that had been on television. In fact, many of them weren't on radio, either, until I got the network started in 1946.

I grew up as a KU fan because my dad was the business manager of athletics when I was a kid. Most people don't realize that. As he was working for Ernie Quigley, Dutch Lonborg, and Phog Allen, I had a pretty good exposure to KU. So, as I was a little kid growing up, I was enamored, particularly, with the basketball team. I followed them closely. I guess you could say I grew into it.

There really wasn't any doubt about where I was going to go to school. As it turned out, I went to school for one year before going into the service for three years. It was an unusual situation, but a lot of us went through the same thing.

When I returned to Lawrence and first started broadcasting, our basketball vantage point was on the first row of the balcony in Hoch Auditorium, where the Hawks played until 1955. We moved in there with all of the fans on my left and on my right and the row behind me. We just sat there with everybody else calling the games. It wasn't an ideal situation, particularly since you had to walk over people to get to the broadcast spot. It wasn't even really blocked off. We had four seats and a little bit of a makeshift wooden platform on which to place our equipment and papers. That was the extent of it.

I remember very clearly the games in Hoch Auditorium, and how the players would walk over from Robinson

Gymnasium, where their locker room was. Doc Allen always had them wear a towel around their heads because he didn't want them to catch cold on their way to Hoch. That walk was about a block. They would walk over to Hoch, which opponents often called the "House of Horrors," because of the circular shape behind the baskets and basically no sidelines. It seated only 3,500, so students had either an A ticket or a B ticket for every other game. Students could not go to the entire home basketball schedule.

Speaking of Doc Phog Allen, there are so many wonderful stories about him. Whenever the team would go back East, Doc was such a dominant figure in college basketball that the media flocked to him. That pressed upon me that we had something special at the University of Kansas. Phog Allen himself was something special. Unlike today's coaches, Doc sought out the media. He loved to be interviewed. In fact, if nobody would come and ask him questions, he'd be terribly disappointed. And, as I pointed out in my book, *A Good Place to Stop*, he always had some dandies. For instance, one of my favorites is when he said, "Our team stood around like Christmas trees — out of season at that." Doc was great. The media loved him, and the feeling was mutual. He loved people, he loved to talk, and he did a pretty good job of it.

Hey! I hear Missouri is a 4-year school now!

Doc was so friendly. He was prominent in the Lawrence community. He was chairman of the Draft Board. When the New York Yankees came to Kansas City to play, they'd get a treatment from Doc because he could make their backs feel better than anyone could in New York. Consequently, he had a hundred stories to tell, and he told every one of them.

Of all the many players who have come through here, Wilt Chamberlain was one of the hardest to get to know, even though we used to host a radio show together. I think he put a shield around himself from way back in his youth because of his size and because he was black. He just really was a private person.

When he came back in 1998 and I presented him to a worldwide audience on CBS that afternoon, he was a different person. He was so touched and moved by the ceremonies and he made a terrific speech, which you can read later in this book. Tears were running down his cheeks. That was one of the most memorable moments from my career. He had not wanted to come back for all of those years because he always thought the KU fans resented him for losing the 1957 National Championship game, the triple-overtime thriller against North Carolina at Municipal Auditorium in Kansas City. I think the fans proved with their thunderous, warm ovation that day that if they ever held it against him, which I don't think anyone did in the first place, all had been forgiven. To see Wilt come out wearing his letter jacket — when most guys' jackets probably would've been eaten by the moths in the basement — was quite a sight. That was an emotional moment. I know it was for him. Wilt concluded his speech with, "Rock Chalk, Jayhawk." That was quite a touching moment.

That moment left an incredible impression on so many people because the Wilt that people had heard about all of those years wasn't the Wilt who was standing before them in Allen Fieldhouse. People who were close to him found him eventually to be a warm, affable guy, unlike his public image.

That also has to be one of the greatest moments in Allen Fieldhouse history. People often ask me, "What is so special about Allen Fieldhouse?" Really, I don't know what it is. It's just the tradition that lurks there. The "Beware of the Phog" sign that hangs in the rafters. It's the smell of the place. It's the history of the place. It's a fun place to be on game night. The "Rock Chalk" chant reverberating through the place when victory is imminent. It's all of those things. Really, it's not as pretty as most of the other places out there today, and the seats are uncomfortable. Strangely, though, I've never talked to a KU fan who wants to build a new arena. Everybody wants to keep Allen Fieldhouse forever and keep it as good as it can be. They're probably right. After all, the fans are one of the reasons it's such a special place.

Unfortunately, when you follow a program for long enough, sometimes you remember the downers as much as the good moments. In 1997, Kansas had arguably the best team in the country, with four starters — Raef LaFrentz, Paul Pierce, Scot Pollard, and Jacque Vaughn — who were headed to the NBA, plus Jerod Haase, who was a great player in his own right and has been an assistant on Roy Williams' staff at North Carolina. Those great players, the All-American kids, lost to Arizona in the Southeast Regional in Birmingham. The Wildcats beat three No. 1 seeds on the way to the National Championship. That regional championship game sticks out as an unforgettable night. It was a night the entire Jayhawk Nation wept.

Overall, I had a wonderful 60 years around the teams, coaches, players, and fans at the University of Kansas. The guys in the athletic department joke with me about knowing everybody in town. I went to Kansas City with Bill Self after the 2009 season. He started his remarks to the group that day about me and how nobody means as much to Kansas athletics as I do. Those kinds of things make an impression on you and make you realize that people appreciate the work I did for 60 years. That's a great feeling.

Like Kirk Hinrich said after I introduced him when KU retired his jersey in March 2009: "Max, I'm so pleased you're here to do this for me. Every great moment that came in my career, you were right there with me." That's nice to hear.

The most incredible reception I've received, though, was during my 60th and final season behind the microphone for the Jayhawks. It started during football. That was the season when KU broke Nebraska's long dominance, dating back to the Orange Bowl team of 1968, with an amazing 40-15 win over the Cornhuskers. That night, Coach Mark Mangino called to see what I was doing Sunday afternoon. He said they would like to have me come to the squad meeting at 3 p.m. in Hadl Auditorium. When I arrived that afternoon, Coach Mangino said they wanted me to have a little something as I wrapped up 60 years of KU football. Believe it or not, it was the game ball from the tremendous win over Nebraska! I wished I knew more of the players well, but it's pretty difficult with football.

Then, I was astounded even more during the basketball season. With nearly each stop in the Big 12, every school except one acknowledged me. (The one was Texas, and their athletic director, DeLoss Dodd, told Lew Perkins that the Longhorns screwed up.) Even our rivals. Kansas State had me come out on the floor and Tim Weiser introduced me. It was right after a technical foul was called on the Kansas State coach, so a few people were booing at first. The cheers soon outlasted the boos. They gave me a Kansas State putter and a nice plaque that mentioned all of the Jayhawk-Wildcat games I'd broadcast. I was certain I'd get boos at Missouri if they introduced me, but I didn't. I received a nice ovation from their fans. The Tigers

Can you read this?

Mizzou Tigers can't.

weren't as courteous — they won the game in overtime. So it went down the line. It was very nice.

For my last game at Allen Fieldhouse, the *Daily Kansan* came out with a huge section and a double-picture of me and the kids all held it up at the beginning of the game and it read: "Thanks, Max!" That was extremely special. Also during that final game at the Fieldhouse, the school retired my number, 60, which was a wonderful moment. Every once in awhile since my retirement I'll glance up and look at that number, which is so far over that it's almost outside. I check on it every so often to make sure it's still there.

Bob Davis

Bob Davis has been calling play-by-play for KU football and basketball for 25 years. Davis, a graduate of Washburn University, is an 11-time Kansas Sportscaster of the Year award winner. In his "free time" during the summer, Davis is an announcer with the Kansas City Royals.

Bob Davis
Photo courtesy of Jeff Jacobsen/
Kansas Athletics

There really isn't an exact moment when I became a KU fan. I spent my junior high and high school years living in Topeka. Before that, when I was in the fifth and sixth grades, we lived in Manhattan, Kansas. So, naturally, I was a little more of a K-State fan as a kid. But I really liked them both and followed both. Living in Manhattan briefly, though, we went to a few K-State games. We could get into games for 50 cents back in those days, so I saw some of those great teams play with guys like Bob Boozer. I'd see them face KU or Missouri, when Norm Stewart was playing for the Tigers. It was fun to do that. That was a great time to be both a K-State and KU fan.

I became more of a KU fan when we were living in Topeka, but there isn't really a specific event that changed me. Growing up and being in the area, we had a lot of relatives in Lawrence that we would visit often. There was something about the Hill. I was always fascinated by the Fieldhouse and Memorial Stadium. I do remember my first game at Allen Fieldhouse. It was in December 1955, Wilt Chamberlain's second home game. The crowd was electric, and Wilt was a man on the court with a bunch of boys. Wilt was involved in the most memorable moment for me in the Fieldhouse, too, but it was a non-game moment. It was in 1998 when he returned for his jersey retirement. That was unbelievable. Everyone had shivers.

KU's football program wasn't as good when I was growing up and then starting to get into the broadcasting business. We'll just say it was a little spotty back then without a lot of consistency, but some of the greatest players of all-time came from KU, particularly Gale Sayers.

I went to college at Washburn in Topeka, and then called Fort Hays State games and area high schools for 16 years. I came into KU a couple of times to fill in for Max Falkenstien, and I also filled in for Tom Hedrick two or three times. One of the times he was sick, so I traveled to Memphis and did the KU-Memphis State game for him. I also filled in on the Missouri schedule for about half of the games in 1983 when John Rooney had other things going — but let's avoid talking about that. By the time Max and I started working together in 1984, we already knew each other, so we just jumped in together and started doing it.

When I got into the business, I liked the announcers at both schools and knew them personally, but I always thought that being the "voice" of the KU Jayhawks would be a really neat thing. There have been so many good announcers come through KU — Max, Tom Hedrick, Merle Harmon, Gary Bender, and Kevin Harlan. There's something about being associated with the state's university that's pretty special. It certainly has been for me.

Kevin Harlan

Kevin Harlan is one of the busiest broadcasters in the business. After being the "voice" of the Kansas City Kings, Kansas City Chiefs, Kansas Jayhawks, and Missouri Tigers, Harlan moved on to network TV with Fox Sports and, since 1998, with CBS Sports. He does everything from NFL to NCAA basketball to the NBA on both radio and TV. Harlan lives in the Kansas City area with his wife, Ann, and their four children.

Kevin Harlan

Photo courtesy of John Filo/ CBS Sports

When I was 10 years old, my dad, Bob Harlan, accepted a job with Dan Devine and the Green Bay Packers. Living in Green Bay from the age of 10 through high school, I never thought I'd end up going to college at the University of Kansas. I was mainly considering the University of Wisconsin and Notre Dame. The one thing I knew is that I wanted to be in broadcasting. Our high school had a radio station, and I was broadcasting all of our games for our high school. (I also was doing some work for commercial stations around the Green Bay area.) So, I was hooked on the trade.

My dad, who at that time was the assistant general manager for the Packers, was in Chicago, where the Packers were playing the Bears. Dad had known Gary Bender for many years. Gary, who's a Jayhawk, used to do radio for the Packers in the mid-1970s. When Dad mentioned to Gary that I was looking at schools, Gary said that I should look at Kansas. "I have a guy down there by the name of Tom Hedrick," Gary said, "who would love to show him around." This was in late December. We got Tom's number. Coincidentally, I had just finished listening to him do the Cotton Bowl for CBS Radio. As I recall, I was frightened beyond belief to meet him. One thing that helped was that Gary called Tom and told him I would be contacting him.

As anyone who knows Tom could imagine, he was very warm and invited me down for a KU game sometime. Later in the month of January, I flew to Kansas City and drove to Lawrence. When I got there, one of the first people I met was Mike Swanson, who went to school there and also had just started keeping statistics for Keith Jackson. I could not believe that. Keith Jackson was one of the guys I'd listened to and tried to emulate — one of my broadcasting idols. The fact that I was standing inside the awe-inspiring Allen Fieldhouse with the guy who kept Keith Jackson's statistics really hit home. (Incidentally, today, Swanee is the Vice President of Communications for the Kansas City Royals.)

This was back in 1978, when Darnell Valentine was a freshman on the basketball team. I sat next to Tom as he was broadcasting the KU-Colorado game. In those days, there was no press row, so the broadcast spot was in the middle of the stands, where the Williams Fund people now sit. I was listening to Tom while watching this Big 8 game between KU and CU.

The next morning I drove back to Kansas City and flew home. When we landed, I told my parents, "I'm going to KU."

During that weekend, Tom told me that if I went to KU, he'd let me do KU baseball with him, but the big thing that shocked me was that he put me on the KU Network to do pregame, halftime, postgame, and sideline reporting during the football games. He and David Jaynes were the broadcast pair. So, I was 18 years old and I was on the KU Radio Network! I couldn't have picked a better school.

I used to fill in for Tom's radio shows and he let me do everything. By doing that, I got an internship at WIBW in Topeka after my freshman year (they usually granted those to people going into their senior year). For four years I did the same thing — football with Tom, baseball with Tom, and his radio shows. That all led to work with the Chiefs and their network, and KCMO in Kansas City. And, right out of college, I found out I was going to get the announcing job with the Kansas City Kings. That was my first job out of college. It's safe to say that Tom Hedrick was as instrumental in my career as anyone. Whenever that stuff happens to you, it always sticks with you. When people give you your first big break, as Tom did with me, you always remember it.

Going to KU for me was just a blast. When I got there, basketball was on a down slope; they were struggling. Across the border, Missouri had Steve Stipanovich and that group, so they were pretty good. The Jayhawks were putting only about 9,000 people in Allen Fieldhouse.

But in football they were good. Kerwin Bell was running the ball and Frank Seurer was the quarterback. David Verser was a wide receiver. They went to the Hall of Fame

Bowl in Alabama. They were really starting to recruit. Football was a bigger deal. I knew the history of KU basketball. I was a freshman when Tony Guy, Mark Snow, and David Magley signed in one Ted Owens trip across the country. I remember thinking how that was really the start of something. My freshman orientation, I was in Wescoe and in the front row sat Tony Guy, David Magley, and Mark Snow. I remember that as if it were yesterday. For whatever reason, though, they struggled for the most part on the court and in the stands. I don't ever recall the fan support being huge for basketball until Larry Brown took over as the head coach.

That couldn't have been more apparent than when I was doing games during Larry Brown's first year, 1983-84, when Kentucky came to Allen Fieldhouse for a December game. The Fieldhouse was sold out. With the exception of maybe a Missouri game, I don't recall seeing Allen Fieldhouse at capacity before that game against Kentucky. The Wildcats had Sam Bowie, Melvin Terpin, Dirk Minniefield, and all those great players. The legendary Cawood Ledford was their broadcaster. KU got beat pretty easily that night, but looking at the sideline there was Brown, with players Ronnie Kellogg, Calvin Thompson, and the like. That Kentucky game was one of those key times when the fans got back into it. I thought that was a huge moment. There was such a buzz because Larry Brown was as good of a coach as there was in basketball. Obviously, he proved everyone right by winning the National Championship in 1988.

Besides Larry himself being here, look at his assistants: John Calipari, R.C. Buford, and Bill Self, just to name three. When Calipari was an assistant for Larry, we used to watch film of different teams in the conference, and then we'd go out for dinner. It was the same for R.C. Buford. I used to do

Larry Brown's radio call-in show on Monday nights, and then we'd get some ribs or steaks and go to R.C.'s house for dinner. I also crossed paths with Self and Bob Hill. But I knew Cal and R.C. as well as I knew anybody there.

What do you call a K-Stater with lots of girlfriends?

A shepherd.

Another person I really enjoyed was football coach Don Fambrough, whom I interviewed each week while I was a student. He was so wonderful, so nice to me. Carole Hadl, John's sister, was Fam's secretary. From the outset, coach treated me like I had been in the business for 40 years. He could not have been kinder to me. He was terrific. I probably have as nice of memories about Don Fambrough as I do any other coach with whom I was associated at KU. He was a wonderful person. He probably doesn't remember me because I was just a student going in his office, but he'd always say in his southern drawl, "Kevin, come on in here." He was very welcoming.

Speaking of John Hadl, I was a ball boy with the Packers when he was a quarterback there. In 1974, Dan Devine traded five draft picks to the Los Angeles Rams in exchange for Hadl. That was a big deal for John to come to Green Bay. In 1973, he led the Rams to the National Conference championship and was the MVP, but he was in his mid-30s and in the last stages of his career.

As I mentioned, the football team at KU when I was a student featured some very good players, especially running back Kerwin Bell. It was electric when he touched the ball because he could fly. Early in his sophomore season in 1981, against Kentucky, Kerwin blew his knee. I was working the sideline for the network, and I got one of the doctors on the air. (They'd never allow this today.) I asked him about Kerwin and he said he had a knee injury. I asked how bad he thought it was, and he said, "He blew his knee. I think he's done." That was a huge deal and from that point on, I couldn't do any more interviews on the sidelines.

A lot of Jayhawks might've forgotten that I spent a few seasons — three to be exact — doing the unimaginable: calling games for the Missouri Tigers. In 1985, after the Kansas City Kings left for Sacramento, I was still with KCMO in Kansas City, and I hooked on with the Chiefs as their play-by-play guy. The summer after my first year with the Chiefs, Missouri had an opening for a broadcaster. Someone at KMOX in St. Louis suggested that I be the new voice for Missouri. They called KCMO, which was the Missouri affiliate in Kansas City. My station didn't have a problem with it, but Norm Stewart, Jack Lingle, Woody Widenhofer, and Joe Castiglione wanted to meet with me before they'd sign off on the deal, because here was a KU guy coming to do Missouri. (Norm, of course, was the basketball coach. Jack, who took over the Marshall football coaching job after their tragedy, was Missouri's athletic director. Woody was an assistant coach, and Joe, who's the AD at Oklahoma, was, at the time, Missouri's director of communications and broadcasting.)

So, in the dead of July, hot as can be, I drove to Columbia and met them at Boone Tavern, a famous restaurant in Columbia. Those guys couldn't have been nicer to me. As it turned out over the years, Norm and I became very good friends to the point that I wrote the foreword for his book. I stayed at Jack's house one night when I missed a connection. I stood in at Joe's wedding. And, I did Woody's farewell for Missouri on the radio. All of those guys, who probably had a lot of second and third thoughts about a KU guy doing their broadcasts, were sold. I stayed there for three years, doing football and basketball. I loved it, which is weird because of my KU ties, obviously.

The St. Louis writers got on me when I would stand for the KU alma mater before games in Lawrence. But that was my school and I was going to stand. I don't know how the Missouri fans took it, but I know the St. Louis writers got a kick out of it and gave me a tough time about it.

Their fans knew I went to KU. I married my wife shortly into that tenure and we started having kids. It took awhile for the Missouri fans to figure out that I was OK. That third and final year that I was there, they could not have been nicer. And Norm Stewart was such a gentleman. I cannot tell you how nice he has been to our family from the time we shook hands in that first meeting. He could not have been nicer in every sense of the word. It became a very positive situation and I enjoyed my three years there very much.

Again, though, there's nothing like your alma mater, especially when that alma mater is the University of Kansas.

As I basically said in Max Falkenstien's book, *A Good Place to Stop*, if you go to that school, any school, whether it's Lipscomb, Wisconsin, or KU, that's how you're identified — always a Bison or a Badger or a Jayhawk. We take great pride in that, but nothing brings out that school spirit and pride as much as winning. Even if you haven't given a lot to that school financially because you didn't attend the school and you're "just a fan," when their teams start to win, you take great pride in it.

At Kansas, when you get Bill Self, Roy Williams, and Larry Brown — three of the biggest names in coaching at any level — as coaches during the past three decades, you see that pride. They've brought KU back to one of the

> **" A lot of Jayhawks might've forgotten that I spent a few seasons — three to be exact — doing the unimaginable: calling games for the Missouri Tigers. "**

five elite basketball programs in the country with Duke, UCLA, North Carolina, and Kentucky. You can't find a better fivesome than that with better history and tradition. When you have so many choices out there, professionally and collegiately, a KU fan is unwavering, deep-seeded, emotional, and passionate, more so than a pro sports fan. There are Missouri fans like that and K-State fans. But, when your team has won and it's recognized as one of the best in a sport, it brings another sense of commitment in terms of how you follow them and how you root for them. It's pretty special. There are Florida Gator fans that are just as passionate about their football team as KU fans are about basketball, so it's not just Kansas. But when you have something like Kansas does with all of those wins, National Championships, history, Allen Fieldhouse, the succession of coaches and the great players who have gone through there and went to pro basketball, I think there's incredible pride. I don't know if the football program will reach that level, because it's hard to be consistently good in both, but KU basketball is something special. Wow!

What great memories. It was so fun. I wouldn't trade my time there for anything.

Mark Stallard

Mark Stallard has been following KU sports most of his life, and writing about sports in general for more than 20 years. The author of 12 books, his titles include the Kansas City Chiefs Encyclopedia, *"Then Landry Said to Staubach...", and* Tales from the Jayhawks Hardwood. *He also has written for numerous sports magazines, the* Wichita Eagle, *and has appeared on the Fox Sports Network's* In Focus. *Stallard currently writes for the website SportsRadioKC.com.*

When most fans think of or hear about the 1968 Kansas football team, it usually has something to do with the Orange Bowl loss to Penn State. And it should. But for me, the things that come to mind are Don Shanklin, listening to games on the radio, the Box Tops rock group, and then, more than anything else, crying. Crying because of a football team, over a football team, for a football team. Crying.

Look through any U.S. history book and you'll find that 1968 was one of the most turbulent, God-awful years America and the world have ever experienced. Horrible assassinations of beloved leaders, deepening war losses in Vietnam, riots in every major city, and racial strife — it was a hard, trying year for most Americans. But for me, a 10-year-old sports fan newbie, 1968 is about a beginning. That's the year my strange, lifelong love affair with KU football began.

Great love affairs — and this one is no exception — usually start with a happy, seductive flirtation.

I listened to the KU-Missouri game at the end of the 1967 season on the radio. My family was at my grandma's house, and Dad went out to the family car to listen to the end of the game. I tagged along, not really knowing what he was doing. He yelled at the radio a couple of times, smiled a few times, and when the game ended — KU won 17-6 — Dad was happy. And I was happy. "Did they win a championship?" I asked. He told me no, but beating Missouri is good, and KU had proved that they were a pretty good team.

I remember thinking, "If they're good, why didn't they win a championship?" I didn't understand the true ramifications of that Missouri game win until years later. The flirtation was done, and I was hooked.

When the 1968 season started, I gladly gave the KU football team my heart.

The Jayhawks steamrolled their first three opponents in 1968, and then beat Nebraska on TV (with only one college game on each week, seeing your team was always a rare treat). At that point in the season I began reading the newspaper game stories, learned who the best KU players were, and started checking the national rankings. KU was in the Top 10, and I knew — just knew! — that a championship awaited the blue-helmeted Jayhawks at the end of the season. And I was certain they would be undefeated.

My favorite Jayhawk player was Don Shanklin, a running back-turned-receiver who also returned kicks and had speed to burn. My dad loved him, so I loved him. When he touched the ball, good things seemed to happen. Maybe I'm wrong, but his name is rarely mentioned when that 1968 team is discussed, and I'm not sure why. Regardless, he was a big part of the team's explosive offense.

Wins over Iowa State and Colorado ran the Jayhawks' record to 7-0. But Oklahoma was the next game. Dad and I had watched the Sooners squeak out a tense, exciting win over Tennessee in the Orange Bowl the previous year, but I didn't know anything about Oklahoma's football prowess and tradition. Of course my dad, who might best be described as an optimistic pessimist or a pessimistic optimist, knew OU's great football history.

"They'll blow it," was a line I heard from him a lot as I got older, and they, whoever the team was, usually did. God love my old man, but if he ever locked in on a team, they seldom disappointed his pessimism.

Because I was only 10 at the time, I opted for unrealistic optimism. It has served me well as a follower of KU football the last four decades.

I was very excited about Kansas playing OU, but I can't remember why. It wasn't on TV, I wasn't going to the game, and since the sports media explosion was still almost 20 years away, the pre-game coverage was limited at best. Somewhere in my decade-old heart, I knew this was the game a season of greatness would be built upon. Kansas hadn't beaten the Sooners in four years, and while OU didn't have the typical unbeatable swagger in their gridiron gait, they were still OU. And a win for KU meant the conference championship was a lock, which meant oranges in January.

Game day was November 9, and I remember nothing about the first half, how the game progressed, even what I was feeling before late in the fourth quarter. I guess tragedy — and I'm using the word loosely here — can sometimes fuzzy up the details. This much I do remember: I was sitting on the bottom bunk bed in my room, with the door closed, listening to the game on my little transistor radio. I mean listening. Imagining the look and feel of the stadium and the game, the uniforms, the weather. I was there. And when KU scored a touchdown with about 10 minutes remaining, it looked like they would win. Then boom, boom, boom, the Sooners scored a late touchdown and took the lead, 27-23. KU made a last-gasp effort to pull out the game, but Ron Jessie dropped a Bobby Douglass pass in the end zone.

The game was over; it was the end of the undefeated dream, the end of all things good and great in my mind, the feeling that nothing about sports was fair.

My team wasn't supposed to lose!

And so I cried. Not much, but enough. A good cry for my defeated team.

Between my tears, I changed radio stations and landed on the Box Tops singing — you guessed it — "Cry like a Baby."

"When I think about the good love you gave me, I cry like a baby ... "

You might think that after the Orange Bowl loss to Penn State (the 12th man game is a different story that meshes into the overall legacy of KU football on many levels) that I cried again. No. That game was more of a stunned disbelief, or as Pepper Rodgers, KU's Coach, said, "We turned a boring win into a thrilling loss."

The week after the loss to OU, the Jayhawks were on TV again, this time against K-State. Fighting through a lackluster performance, KU held off the Wildcats to win, then clinched the Orange Bowl bid the following week against Mizzou, a game I didn't listen to or even think about, something to this day I still don't understand.

Ah, but there is always next year. Next year!

That summer my family took a trip to Florida, and I walked the field at the Orange Bowl, sat in the stands, and had a picture of me and my dad taken under the "Welcome To Miami" sign on the stadium façade. It felt special to be in there, even with the loss to Penn State, and I knew Orange Bowls galore were in the Jayhawks' future.

In 1969, Kansas posted a miserable 1-9 record and was blown out at home on TV by Mizzou, 69-21, in the season finale. By then it didn't matter. I was hopelessly dedicated to the Jayhawks, so much so that when the camera showed a group of students walking around the track carrying a giant banner that read "Kansas will be back," my hope soared.

No more crying for me.

Craig Brown

Craig Brown needed only four-and-a-half years to complete his journalism degree at KU, graduating in December of 1993, which was fine with him because it allowed for more opportunity to call Jayhawk games for KJHK. Today, he's a post-production video editor in Kansas City and writes for several baseball websites, including Royals Authority and the Hardball Times. He lives in Leawood with his wife. Megan (also class of 1993), and their two daughters.

Some time during my sophomore year at KU, in 1991, I hooked up with the campus radio station, KJHK. I began spinning jazz records (yes, even in 1991 we played more wax than CD) and soon realized there was a top-notch news and sports operation that went along with the station.

After a while, I joined the sports staff and paid my dues running the board (or producing as it is technically called) for the sports call-in show that was broadcast on Thursday nights, as well as for a number of games that we broadcast during the week. Since I was edging toward a degree in broadcast news and loved sports, I was in radio heaven.

It was great, how the athletic department handled the student reporters, both for KJHK and *The Kansan*. We had the same access as all the other media. Different rules didn't apply to us just because we were students. Besides the access, the University allowed us to broadcast all home football games, home men's basketball, most of the women's basketball schedule (including the Big 8 tournament, which was always held in Salina, Kansas) and select home baseball games. For us budding play-by-play types, we were always

What do you get when a K-State basketball player sees his shadow?

6 more weeks of bad basketball.

grateful for the opportunity to broadcast big-time college sports.

Football game days at KJHK meant the sports staff owned the airwaves for at least five hours. We began with a one-hour pre-game show, previewing the matchups and featuring some interviews we had collected during the week. Now as the Sports Director of the station, I tried to make KU home football games an event on our airways.

If you were involved in the game-day production, you were expected to be professional. We were aspiring broadcasters, after all! That meant wearing a suit and tie to the football games. (Or as Tom Hedrick, the faculty advisor to the sports staff always put it, "A blue blazer and a power tie!") Once we had collected all our gear at the radio station, we walked down 11th Street to Memorial Stadium. At the stadium, we'd enter the media entrance and hop on the elevator to ride to the top of the press box. The top. The very top. After all these years, I still have no idea where Max Falkenstien and Bob Davis set up for their broadcasts. All I know is we were higher than them. And everyone else in the stadium.

In those days, there were six "floors" to the press box. I think there were some suites on one floor, working media on another, and I have no idea what was on the other floors. At the top of the press box was a floor that was open to the elements. Originally, it was intended for photographers and the scouts to be able to get a bird's eye view of the action. It was in this photo bay that the university built us a platform, so we would be able to have a desktop on which to work while having a seat at the same time. Because it was built off the floor and required a few more stairs for us to get into position, we always told people we worked on floor six-and-a-half. We kind of took a sarcastic pride in having the highest spot in the stadium for the games.

Although we were up in the jet stream, it was really a great place to take in a football game. In September, however, as the season evolved and we moved closer to winter, floor six-and-a-half was an unfriendly place to be. The wind would come in from the north and we were obviously higher than the north bowl of the stadium, so we felt the full force of the bitter gusts. The conditions could be absolutely brutal.

On November 6, 1993, my student broadcasting colleagues and I began our trek to the stadium to broadcast the game against the sixth-ranked Nebraska Cornhuskers. Games against NU were never all that fun. Nebraska, as usual, was rolling through the Big 8 on its way to yet another conference title. Also, the Cornhuskers had beaten KU 24 consecutive times entering that afternoon's contest. The last time Nebraska visited campus, they hung 59 points on an overmatched KU defense. Then there was the fact that Nebraska fans traveled extremely well to away games. The north bowl was always filled with fans wearing red whenever Nebraska came to town. Always.

A couple of hours before kickoff, we made our trek down 11th Street and up to the sixth-and-a-half floor of the press box. As usual for that time of year, it was blustery and bitter. Entering this game, KU was 4-5 on the year, but Nebraska was undefeated, having won at 20th-ranked Colorado the week before. The Cornhuskers had national title aspirations. The Jayhawks were just hoping they could hang around and make the game interesting. As students (and broadcasters), we were hoping for the same thing.

Nebraska was a 16-point favorite heading into the game, but the Jayhawks drew first blood when they took the opening possession and scored on a 30-yard strike from Asheiki Preston to Dwayne Chandler to open a 7-0 lead. It was a great start that really got the crowd pumped and into the game. However, there were some reservations. After all, it was only the first possession of the game. But still, it was nice to have a lead against the Huskers.

As the game evolved, KU's defense was hanging tough against Calvin Jones, Tommie Frazier and Co. However, the Huskers were able to even the score midway through the first quarter before taking the lead in the second. Late in the first half, Nebraska had the ball and was moving seemingly at will. As they marched toward their goal line and Husker fans prepared for the inevitable third score of the half, a strange thing happened. Husker quarterback Brook Berringer (who was in for an injured Frazier) dropped back to throw a pass in the end zone. It was a rare site to see a Nebraska quarterback attempt to throw a pass — they attempted only 12 passes all afternoon against KU. However, the Jayhawk defense was ready and Clint Bowen picked off the pass in the end zone, thwarting the danger and securing just a seven-point deficit heading into halftime.

With the score 14-7 at halftime, the stadium was buzzing. Most of us cynical Jayhawk fans had expected Glen Mason's team to fold much earlier. Yet here they were going toe-to-toe with the big boys of the conference. Up on the sixth-and-a-half floor, we were ecstatic. We had ourselves a ballgame.

In the third quarter, it became clear that the Jayhawk offense was going to ride on the back of their freshman running back, June Henley. Henley announced himself to the Jayhawk faithful a couple of weeks earlier, going for 237 yards in a win against Iowa State. After losing Tony Sands to graduation following the 1991 season (capped off by his memorable 396-yard finale against Missouri), the Jayhawks were in the market for a big-time running back and we all hoped Henley would be the man to fill those shoes. It certainly looked that way when Henley followed up his breakout performance the following week by hanging 178 yards against the 14th-ranked Oklahoma Sooners in a 38-25 loss in Norman.

With Henley powering the offense, the Jayhawks tied the game, 14-14, at the end of the third quarter on a Preston keeper. With just 15 minutes to go, the Jayhawks were somehow — against all odds — in a position to win. The fans were letting the team know how they felt. The crowd was as loud as any I had ever heard at the stadium. What an atmosphere!

As the game remained tight, those of us on the sixth-and-a-half floor were going insane over the airways. As the guy calling the play-by-play for the fourth quarter of the game, I was feeling this was my "signature" moment as a student broadcaster. It's funny to think that because we knew that our audience was miniscule compared to Bob and Max. We didn't care.

Nebraska took the lead midway through the fourth quarter and then Mason and the KU offense turned the game over to Henley. The Jayhawks just pounded the ball down the field, moving 77 yards on 16 plays to put the ball on the three yard line of the Huskers.

When Henley punched the ball into the end zone with less than a minute remaining, Memorial Stadium erupted. Undoubtedly, the roar carried throughout the valley ... hopefully all the way up to Lincoln. KU trailed 21-20.

By this time I was hoarse. It felt like we were talking a mile a minute. "Is Mason going to go for two and the win? He has to go for two! Is he going to go for two?" I was praying that I was making sense (and that the board operator back at the station was rolling tape on my play-by-play).

Sure enough, Mason brought his offense back on the field for what would certainly be the winning margin if the two-point conversion was successful. This was awesome! Mason was known for being fearless and he was backing it up by going for the win.

Then, I noticed something. When Mason sent the offense back onto the field, he kept Henley on the sidelines. Henley, who had shredded the vaunted Nebraska defense for 148 yards, wasn't even going to be on the field for the decisive play of the game. I couldn't believe it.

"June Henley's not on the field!" I shouted into my microphone. "Where's June Henley? Why in the world would you run a two-point conversion and not have KU's biggest offensive threat on the field?"

I couldn't believe that Mason would leave his offensive star on the sidelines. Even if he didn't want to be predictable and give him the ball, at least put him on the field to give the defense something to think about. KU ran the ball 50 times that afternoon, with 37 of those carries going to Henley. He was the only back that was able to do anything positive against the Husker defense. He HAD to be in the game. Only, he wasn't.

The Jayhawks did run a play-action, but the Huskers didn't bite and Preston's pass fell incomplete in the corner of the end zone. Game over.

After the game, the media quizzed Mason about playing for the win instead of the tie. When did he decide to go for two? "When I first took this job and saw what a lopsided series it was," was Mason's answer.

I always felt it was absolutely the right call to go for two. KU, in the middle of the pack of the Big 8, had nothing to lose. Sure, a tie would have hurt the Huskers' title aspirations, but Mason didn't give a damn about that. All he wanted was to win the game for the Jayhawks and break that streak.

Now, almost 20 years later, I look back at the box score from that afternoon and marvel at how well Mason's team played. They had 19 first downs (the same number as NU) and held the ball for 30:19. They had only three penalties (again, the same as the Huskers) and didn't turn the ball over once.

It was the perfect game for the Jayhawks. Only the result was imperfect.

Bob Jensen

Bob Jensen graduated from KU with a degree in accounting in 1970. He has been a season-ticket holder to KU football games for 38 years, and to Jayhawk basketball games for five years. He was Director of Finance for Metropolitan Community College in Kansas City for 26 years.

My KU story has to do with when we lost to Penn State in the 1969 Orange Bowl. Most KU fans remember that as the infamous 12th man game that the Jayhawks probably should've won. For me it means a lot more. It happens to be the day that I left Vietnam to come back home. I was about the only one on the flight who was thrilled that the plane was late to get us. It allowed me to listen to the Orange Bowl in Vietnam before heading home. Though I was sad that the Hawks had to lose the game, I was thrilled that I was headed home.

Bob Jensen and family.
Photo courtesy of Bob Jensen

I started following KU in both football and basketball when I began junior high school in 1958. My sister, who is six years older than I am and went to KU, is probably part of the reason I liked the teams. Plus, at that time, the Jayhawks had this 7-foot basketball player from Philadelphia named Chamberlain who was completely unstoppable. Unfortunately, back then, we did not get to see many games on TV so we had to rely on the radio. The football team was even pretty good back then in their powder blue uniforms. John Hadl was quarterback and Curtis McClinton was a big running back that could not be stopped. When they added Bert Coan, they really had one of the best backfields that I have seen at KU.

Those guys were among my favorites, plus Nolan Cromwell. I remember seeing him excel at both safety and quarterback. I would love to see him be considered as the next KU coach when Mark Mangino decides to leave. John Riggins was another Kansas farm boy who could just not be stopped. He was sort of a different kid with his curly hair, but he could not be stopped when he was running up the middle of the line. Of course, an electrifying runner was Tony Sands, who had some great long runs. I'll never forget his game against Missouri when he racked up 396 yards. Having it happen against the Tigers made it that much sweeter.

There have been so many memorable football games during my time following the Jayhawks, through both the lean years and the recent years of resurgence. I seem to remember a game, I believe in 1973, when we played K-State in Lawrence. This was back in the days when we did not have the huge scoreboard with the video board. There were temporary bleachers in the south end, and it was a big deal to watch a game from the Hill. In this particular game, the entire Hill was covered with fans. We were in for a treat. It was one of the best games from simply a game standpoint. The lead seemed to go back and forth between the two teams. Fortunately, KU was the last one to score and won the game. I've thought since then — and even today —that it was too bad anyone had to lose. (Of course, I'm glad K-State did, though.)

Speaking of "back in the day," before Memorial Stadium had lights and "band day" was during the afternoon, it always seemed to fall during a September game, which could be extremely hot. At that time, the band members had traveled from far away and they wore their full band uniforms, which were very thick and heavy. There used to be this doctor who would cruise around in a golf cart, wearing a 10-gallon white hat and a white suit. He would look after the band members as they collapsed from the heat. I remember always thinking "Why don't they just wear T-shirts?!"

Because Memorial Stadium didn't have fixed lights, when the Hawks did play night games, they had to rent portable lights. It used to be so dark when you would walk down the steps to leave the stadium. The only lights that were available to help were just a single light bulb hanging from a long cord. It was like lighting the steps with a candle.

When it comes to basketball, it is difficult to keep my list of favorites to just a couple. Mark Turgeon is at the top of the list when it comes to pure effort. His story of going from walk-on to helping lead the Jayhawks to a Final Four to developing into a good head coach, is inspiring. Danny Manning is obviously one of the greatest players in KU history, but he's also a class guy and a fantastic coach. And, I can't leave out Kirk Hinrich and Ron Kellogg.

What's better than a Missouri fan?

A dead Missouri fan!

The only player I used to talk to much was Rex Walters when he played with the Kansas City Knights of the ABA. They practiced at Penn Valley Community College. At that time, I was the Director of Finance at the Metropolitan Community College, and would use our fitness center at Penn Valley. Rex would also be using the fitness center and I would talk to him since he had graduated with one of my sons, Todd, with a degree in education.

My only other meeting and talking with former players was when I was at a conference at Disney World and Patrick Richey was there with his wife, who worked at UMKC. While we were there, KU was in the Sweet 16, so we all headed to the ESPN Zone to watch the game. It was very cool to hear Patrick talk about things during the game, including some of the things the coaches would be saying on the bench and in the huddle during timeouts.

When talking about favorites from KU, though, one near the top for so many people has to be Max Falkenstien. I've had the chance to talk to Max when he signed both of his books for my two sons, Todd and Jeff. Max is really a class guy who was so much fun to listen to on the radio for all of those years. And what a dream job to broadcast the Jayhawks for 60 years!

I've loved watching so many of the coaches from Pepper Rodgers, Glen Mason and Mark Mangino in football to Larry Brown, Roy Williams and probably the best of the group, Bill Self.

Speaking of coaches, I've always remembered Roy's annual quote: "Just enjoy the ride." For more than 50 years, thanks to the Jayhawks, I've done just that.

I have been a football season-ticket holder ever since graduating from KU. The Jayhawks are great to watch these days. A far cry from some of the teams we've had. There have been many, many Saturdays when the band at Memorial Stadium was definitely the highlight of the day!

But, it has really been a fantastic ride over all of the years being a Jayhawk. Thanks for giving me the opportunity to reflect back on some of my more memorable moments in KU history.

CHAPTER 2

Kansan By Birth, Jayhawk By the Grace of God

Steve Beaumont

Steve Beaumont (Class of 1986) was a KU Yell Leader from 1983-86. He is the father of three big Jayhawk fans, Colton, Shelby and Ethan. He owns the Chateau Avalon Hotel, Health Specialists, Inc., and a commercial real estate development company.

Steve Beaumont
Photo courtesy of Steve Beaumont

As a yell leader for four years at KU, I have enough stories to fill an entire book. I was there at an interesting time: Larry Brown's first few years, a trip to the Final Four, basically bad football teams, and the start of a few cheers that are still going strong today. And it seems like most of the things happened during 1984-85.

The first that comes to mind is something that I understand Calvin Thompson points out: the "Woooosh!" sound from fans when a KU player hits his free throws. In 1984-85, we had a game in Washington, D.C., against George Washington University. My cheering partner, Debbie Saggau, was talking to the KU athletic director, Monte Johnson, and KU had decided at the last minute to take four cheerleaders to the game. They went (I had studies and couldn't go). It was a pretty normal game. No stories I know of, but one thing did stick and is now a KU tradition. When the other team (George Washington) went to shoot a free throw, their crowd went quiet, and then if the ball went through the hoop there was a thunderous "Woooosh!" One of our cheerleaders thought that was so cool that she got me to start doing it at our games at Allen Fieldhouse using my megaphone. Roger Nelson and Rhonda Strobble, the partners next to us on the court, did it with us. The rest is history, so to speak. Whenever I do the Woooosh! with my kids at Allen Fieldhouse now and see 15,800 other rabid KU fans WOOOOSHING in unison, I wonder if they would believe me if I ever told them how this started.

That was also the season we started the "da daaa da, HEY, da da da … da daaa da, HEY, da da da … we're gonna beat the … " well, you know the rest. It's a chant that is now ubiquitous at all college and professional events, it seems. But I can tell you prior to 1984-85 no one in this part of the country ever heard of it. I don't know that KU created it, but I can tell you that I had certainly never heard it at any event or seen it on TV anywhere prior to it starting at KU. The story goes like this. Ron McCurdy was the Pep Band Director at this time. He was an exceptional musician and Pep Band instructor. He even was friends with Bobby McFerrin of "Don't Worry Be Happy" fame.

I was the captain of the Cheer Squad and in the early fall of that year, during the football season, Ron had a meeting with me to tell me the music and cheers he would like to work on with us for the upcoming basketball season. He had some new fight songs that he wanted us to create routines and pyramids for. We sat in his office and he played me a number of songs the Pep Band had recorded onto a tape for us. About the fifth song in, he started with an explanation. He said this was a song from the 1970s by Gary Glitter. "On this song you (cheerleaders) only have one job," he said, "coax the crowd to scream HEY at a few points during the song." We then listened to the song and Ron animatedly shouted HEY at the appropriate points. I thought it sounded OK but wondered what the heck the crowd would make of it.

A few weeks later I played the same tape for the squad with my co-captain, Nicki Hoffman. When we explained the HEY and that we would do some stunt and just have the cheerleaders raise their arms simultaneously with the HEY, the looks were bordering on yawns. Most were like my first impression — all we do is a simple stunt, raise our arms, and shout HEY and the crowd is supposed to get excited? This was the era of dangerous, three-high pyramids and mini-tramp routines (both of which were banned within three years because of accidents). Our fear was that the crowd wouldn't care a lick.

Nonetheless, we introduced the HEY cheer during the start of the regular season. It pretty much landed with a dud. The looks on the faces of the crowd told the story. They expected a song they were used to: "I'm a Jayhawk," "Stand Up and Cheer," or even "Sunflower Song." What was this new simpleton cheer? Ron, to his credit, believed in the cheer and said it would remain on the playlist. We continued to do our best to coax the crowd into a rousing HEY. We couldn't find the exact right time to get the song into the flow so that it worked with the crowd.

> For some reason, Proctologists are attracted to Lincoln...

I can't remember the game, but it was around January. The Hawks were playing well; it was obvious that Coach Brown was building a consistent winner. Sellouts were back consistently and the vibe was palpable in Allen. In this particular game, we were playing a national non-conference power team in a back-and-forth contest. Sometime in the first half, I remember a string of about 60 seconds where our defense was stifling them and we were converting on the other end with transition buckets and alley-oops to Calvin Thompson. You could feel the energy building. In the period of a minute, we went from a tied game to something near a double-digit lead.

Then it happened. Ron played HEY instead of "I'm a Jayhawk" or "Sunflower Song." The crowd sprung to its feet and, in one riotous outburst, rattled the rafters of Allen with HEY. I thought dust would come falling off those old beams that held up the ceiling. It was such a hit we played it again at every opportunity when a timeout was called or when we had seized momentum. It was something of a cheerleading/Pep Band crescendo. At a timeout, Ron and I would catch eyes across the court and give each other the sign for HEY if we thought the moment was right. We now had a cheer that was downright intimidating. The funny part is in hindsight I can't recall any middle ground. The KU students were always supportive of our cheers. The old-line alums were a tougher egg to crack. On that winter day in early 1985, three generations finally agreed that they could express themselves with one simple word: HEY.

We all but owned the HEY cheer for a little more than a year. I didn't hear it anywhere else we traveled. Then after the end of the school year in 1986, KU's Final Four team was invited to attend a Kansas City Royals game. And guess what they played during a rally? HEY ... at a Royals game. What the heck? The Royals? I wasn't sure if I was flattered or offended. What's next? "I'm a Jayhawk" at Chiefs games? Then the insult. In 1987, when I was watching a KU-MU game from Columbia, I heard the Tigers doing it. Now that was cold. What a bunch of copycats! Now it seems that every junior high through professional team uses HEY as their rousing adrenaline burst cheer. Did KU start it? Only Ron McCurdy would know. I can tell you this: If you notice at these events that it isn't Gary Glitter's version, it's probably an arrangement much more similar to that of the KU Pep Band in 1985 created by Ron McCurdy.

Not all new cheers make it, though. In 1984-85, I was called to the athletic offices at the request of legendary KU track Coach Bob Timmons. Bob said that he and some of his track athletes noticed that we had a mythical bird mascot but it made no sound. He wanted us to start a cheer where we would make the sound of a Jayhawk. I was dumbfounded but asked what that sounded like. Bob took a breath and then, "Wawk, Wawk … Wawk, Wawk … " done to a hand-clapping beat. Then during the Wawk parts you put your five fingers together to form the head of a Jayhawk, and then open the fingers from the thumb for each Wawk, Wawk. Bob talked to the Pep Band and Ron McCurdy, who created a drum backbeat for the cheer. Oh, you haven't heard the Wawk, Wawk cheer? For good reason. It died a merciful death in less than two games, never to be heard from again. OK, so not all cheers can be winners.

Maybe we should've tried the Wawk, Wawk cheer at Oklahoma. It might've gone over better than I did with Sooner basketball Coach Billy Tubbs. In 1984, I believe, we were playing OU at Lloyd Noble Arena on a nationally televised weeknight game. Cameras everywhere. This is back in the day when opposing teams could actually bring six to eight cheerleaders on the road. In this case we were, for some reason, put closest to the OU team bench. That would come to haunt me.

It's late in the first half. KU fouls an OU player and sends him to the line for two shots. He made the first and, like I always did, I pounded my megaphone on the court to make a little noise. On the road, particularly in Norman in the 1980s, cheerleaders were the only support our guys had. The

Sooner player started to shoot the second shot and just as he did, I lifted my megaphone to my mouth and shouted REBOUND! He made the shot but then the wheels fell off.

Before we could inbound the ball, Billy Tubbs stopped play and was stomping his feet right in front of me pointing at me and shouting at the refs. He just kept screaming at them and gesticulating at me. I was freaking out. What is happening? It went on for what seemed like forever, Tubbs fuming. I finally heard him say, "I want him outta here," followed by the international ejection signal to the lockers. In my case I think he wanted me out of the building entirely. Finally he went back down the bench, sat and leered at me, his comb-over out of place.

One of the refs came over to me with a serious look on his face. I was frozen. As he got up to me, his face lightened and he touched my shoulder and said "Coach Tubbs doesn't want you to yell anymore." He was almost holding back a laugh. I said "But I'm a yell leader!" He said, "Just cool it when they are shooting free throws, OK?" I said "No problem," and was like a mouse in church from that point on.

I can't recall if we won that game but one thing is for sure: Billy Tubbs kept his home-court advantage and added to his legend. I, on the other hand, got TV time I did not want and still get chills remembering it. Note to self: in Lloyd Noble, yell leaders are better seen and not heard.

There was a stretch of about three months in the fall of 1985 that I'll never forget, largely because of the basketball team and, in particular, Danny Manning.

It started off in September when we were practicing in Allen Fieldhouse. The basketball team hadn't officially started practicing yet, but players were in there nearly every day playing pick-up games. At the time, the bleachers were put away and we were practicing on the cinder track that used to go around the basketball floor. Things were pretty loose and I knew several of the basketball players, so I'd be talking to them while we were practicing different tricks. At the end of practice, I decided I wanted to try an acrobatic stunt on the mini-trampoline. We had 16 cheerleaders and yell leaders there that day, eight women and eight men. Each one stood in a line and bent over at the waist. I put the trampoline on one end and a big mat on the other end. (You can see where this is going.) I came boring down and did a flip off the tramp over all of them. That was for fun, not for show.

> One of the refs came over to me with a serious look on his face. I was frozen. As he got up to me, his face lightened and he touched my shoulder and said, 'Coach Tubbs doesn't want you to yell anymore.'

Danny saw me do it. We were already pretty much packed up and ready to leave. He said, "Hey, do that again! These guys didn't see that!" He got his buddies and I thought it was cool that they wanted to watch. So, I did it again. Instead of landing on my feet and running out of it, though, I landed short and my body froze when I landed. The shock went straight up my leg. I knew I was hurt, but with the basketball players high-fiving me, I didn't say anything. For the next week my leg kept hurting. It got progressively worse to where I couldn't walk around campus. Ronnie Kellogg sat next to me in a religion class and I asked him what he thought might be wrong. He told me to go see the trainer. The trainer sent me to the team physician. They scheduled me to go in for arthroscopic surgery.

On the day of the surgery, they said they'd be done in an hour and I'd be home in two hours. Oops. I woke up and had

How does a
K-State
football fan
count to 10?

0-1, 0-2,
0-3, 0-4...

this long cast on and tubes coming out with blood. When they went in they found out I fractured my leg straight up the middle of the femur. They had to cut out my broken femur and then left my knee cap detached so the femur could heal correctly. The only good thing is that I got to watch the start of the Royals-Toronto (baseball) playoffs from my bed at the Lawrence Memorial Hospital ... thanks to Danny Manning telling me to try that one more time.

To this day, I don't even think Danny knows I did that. After all, how many times does a basketball player miss a yell leader?

Remember the Billy Tubbs story? Although it was my most memorable, that wasn't the only trip to Norman that stands out. The other was in November 1985, about a month after my surgery, when the football team traveled to play the Sooners. OU was a national power, as usual. Just one year earlier, though, they came to Lawrence ranked No. 2 in the polls and the Jayhawks pulled off the ultimate upset of my time at KU by beating them, 28-11, at Memorial Stadium.

We went to OU in 1985 with a little ray of hope of beating them, but we were nonetheless realistic. Winning in Norman isn't easy. Prior to leaving Lawrence, our Spirit Squad coordinator gave me the itinerary for our Saturday pre-game festivities. Since I wasn't fully healed, my main duties were to drive the van and carry our boom box for the recorded music. The normal game day for a cheerleader starts early with at least one pep rally for alums. In this case, we had not one event to attend, but three. The first was an alumni rally at the same hotel where we were staying, so no problem there. We got up early, and performed two or three fight songs with a small group of the marching band providing the music.

The second rally was at a Norman golf country club. Strangely, it was attended by some KU alums, but mostly it was OU fans in attendance. This time, we were sans band and performed to our own tape-recorded music. It's always interesting to have to hit the play button then run across the room in time to throw a girl in the air for the first eight-count of music. Luckily, with hop-along there, I hit play and then watched. I recall this event as being fun and memorable but not as much as our next stop.

All I had on the itinerary was "Steve Owens Luncheon," followed by an address. It was in the same area as the country club we were already in. So we drove the van to the address. To our surprise it was a private residence, and no ordinary residence, at that. It was the home of Steve Owens, the famed OU football standout and Heisman Trophy winner. The cheerleaders were all wondering why the heck this was on our itinerary for the morning.

Nothing like this had happened before. I don't know why it happened. My guess was that Steve Owens liked to entertain at his home for home games and the opposing team's cheer squad would certainly be good entertainment. If I had to guess, I'd bet he made a donation to the KU athletic department for the appearance and probably did so with other schools. But that's just a guess.

I knocked on the door and Steve Owens himself opened it and cordially welcomed us all into his home. As you would expect, the cheerleaders were taken straight to the OU alums in attendance, while we yell leaders did our best to blend into the walls of the home. Not easy when you are wearing polyester crimson, blue, and white from head to toe. I got a plate of food and along with Roger Nelson, a fellow yell leader, slipped into the den to sit down and eat. I sat right next to Owens' imposing fireplace. It was devoid of any decoration except one thing: right in the middle was his Heisman Trophy. I immediately put down my food and stood up to admire it. Upon closer inspection, I noticed the arm was broken. That famous "stiff arm" that is out in front to push away would-be tacklers was somehow pulled in two. From the elbow to the shoulder, part of it was pointing down while the rest of the arm was in its normal pose. Surely there should be some kind of warranty on this statue, right?

The OU alums were completely cordial and fascinated by us. Truth told, the wives did spend a lot of time talking to the yell leaders, but nothing like the men and our cheerleaders. It was a great experience, though.

After finishing our meal we were invited out back to do some KU fight songs and entertain the OU fans in attendance. Then it was off to the football game. By the time we got there, the lot for our parking pass was full, so the parking attendants moved us off to a grassy field in the middle of thousands of OU tailgaters. Needless to say, getting from our van into the stadium meant enduring some interesting comments, most of them ogling at our cheerleaders. It's important to note that one of the job descriptions for a yell leader is to serve as bodyguard for the cheerleaders and dancers. Sometimes I wonder if that is the main reason they keep us around.

Anyway, the game didn't go our way. OU handled KU pretty easily and gave us payback for the year prior. Then it was time for our trek back to our van among the legion of OU fans. We made it without incident, although I think at least two cheerleaders had engagement offers along the way. When we got near where we'd parked the van, we saw the same OU alums tailgating that we saw on the way in. They were a bit surprised to see us, though I couldn't figure out why. A few more steps and I found out why. Our van was gone!

This was in the era before cell phones so it meant me going back into the stadium to find an official or phone to try and track down who had towed or stolen our van. The rest of the squad stayed with the OU alums while I went back by myself to seek help. Eventually, I found a parking official who could track down what had happened. Apparently, someone decided to tow our van to the correct lot after all! It would have been nice if someone had told us. By the time I got back to the squad they were surrounded by OU fans and everyone was laughing, having a great time. We ended up staying around with that group for probably more than an hour before finally going to find our van.

That was a pretty memorable trip to Norman, and certainly made up for my encounter with Billy Tubbs the previous year.

The last event of that crazy two-month stretch came three weeks after the OU game when the Jayhawk basketball team went to New York to play in the 1985-86 preseason NIT at Madison Square Garden. We ended up playing Louisville and Duke right after Thanksgiving. The trip was incredible, made even more fun by walking the streets of the city with the likes of Calvin Thompson, Ron Kellogg, and some other Jayhawks. Very cool. In the first game, KU played Louisville.

The two best cheerleading squads in the country, for quite some time, have been Louisville and Kentucky. That year was no exception. Louisville had two All-America yell leaders. Somehow, we got in a handstand contest with these guys during halftime. The cool thing was that the crowd was getting in to it. I did a handstand on top of Roger Nelson's hands. Louisville, with James Speed on top, did the same thing on top of a guy named Andre. Soon, the crowd was starting to clap and make noise when they realized it was now an endurance competition. I looked over and could see Speed turning red. Finally, he gave up and fell down. I did handstand pushups to the crowd's enthusiasm. We got an incredible ovation ... at Madison Square Garden! That same game, the Bud Light Daredevils were there and two of their guys were former K-State yell leaders. I knew them and asked them if I could do a couple tricks with them. So, I got to perform with them, which was cool. Looking back now, though, I'm not sure why I never got in trouble for that. But, that's an unforgettable trip from being around the basketball team to getting an ovation at the famous Madison Square Garden.

One great thing about being a yell leader in the mid-1980s was just the fact that KU basketball was gaining incredible popularity again under new Coach Larry Brown. He even respected the cheerleaders. I invited him to a taco party one time at my apartment at 10th and Mississippi. Some of the cheerleaders didn't even show up, but Larry Brown came by! He didn't stay long enough to have any tacos, but he wanted to make an appearance and tell everyone hello. While he was there, he took time to talk to us. He had horn-rimmed glasses and was very soft-spoken. It felt a little like talking to Woody Allen. Coach had this uncle kind of feel to him. Well, an uncle with a great basketball mind. He was so different from the loud Coach Brown I saw at practice who totally commanded his players. At this time, the cheerleaders and yell leaders were allowed to be in the Fieldhouse when the team was practicing. So I got to see Coach Brown in action. It was uncanny the things Coach

Brown could remember about games, right down to possessions.

During Coach Brown's first year there, I had read somewhere that he was Jewish. So, in December I got him a Happy Hanukkah card, which the cheerleaders signed. I handed it to Coach during pregame warm-ups. He just glanced at the envelope and put it in his pocket. Before the game, he evidently had time to open it because he came over and said, "Thank you. How did you know?" I had fun with that.

> What are the best 4 years of a Mizzou student's life?
>
> 3rd grade.

In many ways, Coach Brown rubbed off on one of his students, Bill Self. From the second he became KU's coach, I've been excited. Excited about the type of coach he is — adaptable and respectable come to mind, excited about the teams he will put on the court, and excited about the type of person he is. That became especially evident to me during the fall of 2006. A few months earlier, KU lost to its second "B" team, Bradley. I was reading the message boards about all of the bad things people were saying about Bill Self. I sent him a note with a scripture in it and told him I thought he was doing a great job and, as an alum, I was proud of him. I also gave him an invitation to the Chateau Avalon for he and his coaches. I didn't hear anything back, which was fine.

In August, I got a letter from the KU basketball office. Seemed odd, but it turned out to be a fold-out card inviting me to join Coach and his wife at their football suite for a game in September. I couldn't figure out why in the world he would invite me to his suite. Did he think I was some high-rolling alum who would donate millions for a new facility? Did they really think I was rich? I kept thinking about it, and actually contemplated not going. It would be easier to decline than to sit there and have to tell him that I couldn't make that type of donation. A few weeks later I decided to go and I would just tell them I couldn't help.

My wife and I got to Memorial Stadium, and as we were getting ready to go up to the suite, here comes Bill Self with a cooler, wearing jeans and a pressed shirt. We gave each other that "man hi" — nod of the head. We got up to the suites, went in and he immediately turns and says, "Hey, are you Steve Beaumont?" I said yes, but I was shell shocked. He was as friendly as can be. He introduced me to the other people in the suite, including all of his coaches. Meanwhile, his wife, Cindy, took my wife over and introduced her to the coaches' wives. I was waiting for the other shoe to drop. But, no, Bill Self asked me to sit down next to him. He wanted to talk about business and being an entrepreneur as much as I wanted to talk about basketball. During the second half, when the shoe hadn't dropped, I said to Bill, "Can I ask you a question? Why am I here?" He couldn't believe it. He said, "Last year, my first year, we had this suite and we never used it. I told Cindy after we lost to Bradley that I was going to invite people to this suite that I want to get to know." I couldn't respond. I was absolutely floored. I never felt unwelcome that day. Quite the contrary. Coach Self is as genuine of a man as you can be. He's the real article.

All of these things that have happened to me at the University of Kansas were like dreams come true. I've been blessed. I've loved KU since the fifth grade. In fifth grade, I was a successful track guy. Our track coach took us to the KU Relays. I can distinctly remember, in about 1975, the Relays were THE thing. The stands were probably 60 percent full with palpable excitement. World-class athletes were there. My favorite memory was seeing this guy from KU who didn't use starting blocks. He used a three-point stance. Come to find out, it was Nolan Cromwell. He blew everyone away. I found out he was also a football player, and he played both offense and defense for the Jayhawks. I started going to KU football games because of him. He got me stoked about KU. We went to the Relays again in the sixth grade. At that time, my Uncle Dennis was there. He was at Jayhawk Towers and we walked over to the Fieldhouse to see my first game. I was hooked then. Goosebumps. I can say, from that first game, throughout my entire collegiate career, to even today, I can't walk inside the Fieldhouse without getting goosebumps. There's a tremendous awe and history every time I go in there. I have a feeling that as long as Bill Self is the basketball coach, those goosebumps will continue.

Juan Heath

Juan Heath is a lifelong Kansas resident. He attended the University of Kansas for seven years, from 1993 to 2000. He met his wife at KU, and they frequently attend football, men's and women's basketball, and baseball games with their young children.

I've been a Jayhawk all of my life. Growing up in Kansas, I've never known anything else. I started attending the Midwest Music Camp when I was in junior high school, and did it every summer until I was a KU student.

Being KU fans somewhat reverberates around our lives. I met my wife at KU. Her dad went to school there, so she and her two sisters are second-generation Jayhawks. At our wedding, the guys wore red ties and red vests, while the girls wore blue dresses and carried sunflowers. I really wanted a mascot at the reception, but my wife drew the line at that.

I was a student at KU from 1993-2000, the end of the Glen Mason years and the beginning of Terry Allen. I played in the marching band, but I wasn't a huge football fan. Like many in the marching band, you pay your dues, so to speak, by doing the football games so you can get tickets to the men's basketball games. At least that's how it was when I was in school there. I was in the band for only two years, so I missed going to the Aloha Bowl on KU's tab. I've regretted that ever since.

Upon graduation, I moved to Florida to work for a newspaper there, and had the good fortune to attend the Tangerine Bowl when KU played North Carolina State. I became so impressed, not only with the improvement of the team, but Coach Mark Mangino, especially. His story of a blue-collar, hard-working background speaks to me about what he's been through, and now he's risen to prominence. In fact, if I had to pick a favorite Jayhawk, it'd be Coach Mangino.

So, I started attending games with a friend of mine from KU, Chris Fickett. He took me to my first road game of the Mangino era, when we went to Evanston, Illinois, to watch the Jayhawks play Northwestern. One thing that struck me about that game is that there were so many KU alumni from the Chicago area. I've heard there were 8,000-10,000 KU fans there. All I know is that we were big enough and loud enough to cause their quarterback, in their home stadium, to have an offside penalty, twice. There was that much noise. It was impressive.

I started getting addicted to traveling the country to see the KU football team's road games. The element that I enjoy in particular is that you get to meet and learn more about the players' families. At home, they don't really stand out as much. I met Charles Gordon's mom at the Fort Worth Bowl.

(She told me, in her motherly way, that she wished Charles would've stuck with baseball because she was afraid he'd get hurt playing football.) I've sat with Scott Webb's father on a couple of occasions, including a road trip I took to Lubbock, Texas. This is a story on its own.

I had attended 24 consecutive KU football games, home and away, from the Tangerine Bowl to the Fort Worth Bowl. But, I couldn't find anybody who would drive to Lubbock with me, and airfare was too expensive, so in order to go to Lubbock, I actually rode a Greyhound bus. My wife took me to Lawrence, where I caught the bus. There was a connection in Oklahoma City and another in Amarillo, Texas. Everything was uneventful on the way down. I got to Lubbock around 6:00 in the morning. I accidentally stumbled upon the KU team hotel, so I got a room there. I visited with some of the players' families during the day, walked around the campus — which is another reason traveling with the team can be interesting. Coming back, though, things on the trip went horribly wrong. There were supposed to be two busses leaving Lubbock but only one showed up. I ended up getting re-routed through Dallas, where I rented a car. I actually drove back with a stranger. I hadn't had a good night's sleep in a couple of days, so I was worried about driving back by myself. So, I picked up a gal who was traveling with her young son to central Missouri. We arranged for me to take her to Kansas City, and her family would pick her up there and take her to central Missouri. As it turned out, we found out on the way that they couldn't pick her up, so I had to detour to Camdenton, Missouri, in the Ozarks. I got lost in the Ozarks and went through Columbia, of all places!

I've been to all of the bowl games of the Mark Mangino era. I've been to 10 of the Big 12 stadiums, including

Memorial Stadium. (I've been to all Big 12 stadiums during my life, just not during Mangino's era.) Having been to some of the horrible defeats and ugly losses, all those made me appreciate being in Miami at the Orange Bowl when Kansas defeated Virginia Tech. The highs are so much more higher than the lows are low. It's been great to watch this transformation of Kansas football and Kansas football fans. It's no longer "just" a basketball school. A quote that I use a lot from Mangino is about how the days are over of Kansas being one-dimensional. The school is good in a lot of things and the fans want us to be good in a lot of things. That has continued in baseball and women's basketball and so on. I'm a proud fan, but out of my love for the University of Kansas, it's wonderful to have this swagger.

My son is somewhat short in stature. So much so that the doctors were a little concerned and wondered if they should send him to a specialist. My response to the doctors has been, "Well, Todd Reesing is big enough." I've shared that story with Todd Reesing's dad. He got a kick out of it.

Here is one of the favorite stories in my life, not just as a Jayhawk. My grandma, Betty McCord, was a big Kansas Jayhawk fan, but she'd never been to a game at Allen Fieldhouse. Kirk Hinrich was her favorite player because of his work ethic. She used to say how he was a "hard-working little fella."

So, when I saw that he was returning in March 2009 for his jersey retirement ceremony, I wanted to figure out how I might get her to that game. It came down to the 11th hour. A friend of mine in the athletic department helped me get a couple tickets a day or two before the game. I went up early on game day and exchanged those tickets for wheelchair seating behind the goal at Allen Fieldhouse. My grandmother was born in Missouri but was a lifelong Kansas fan. Her exact words on moving to Kansas were, "I got the hell out as fast as I could." She was from the Ozarks, but a big believer in the University of Kansas, and a big believer in KU Medical Center.

In fact, a side story about that. She was admitted to the ER a few years back. She was confused at first and started to become a bit agitated, telling everyone that she wanted to be taken to KU Med. My family and I finally stepped out into the hallway and grabbed a staff person and showed Grandma this person's identification badge with the Jayhawk on it. Once she saw that, she settled down and realized she was in the hospital that she thought so much of.

I took her to the Booth Hall of Athletics before the game at Allen Fieldhouse. She got to soak in all of the pregame atmosphere and festivities. She told me at one point, "I thought it'd be louder for the Border War." I was concerned the sound would bother her because it was so loud, but obviously it didn't.

When they brought Kirk Hinrich out for the ceremony, she had a grin from ear to ear. She loved every moment of that. We stayed for the whole game. My wife and children made a sign for her to take to the game. The sign read: "It's my first KU game." We met a few of the players afterwards and they autographed it for her. Adding to the experience, someone I've never met posted their personal pictures from that game on a KU website. In one of the photos, clearly in the background, under the basket, you see my grandmother in her red coat, with me next to her, pulling for the Jayhawks. Then, while picking up my daughter from basketball camp a few months after that game, there's a panoramic shot of that game. Sure enough, plain as day, there's my grandmother! Her image is captured for all-time for every Jayhawk fan who gets that photo. For her first KU game, to me that's pretty awesome.

My grandmother passed away in the summer of 2009, about three months after going to that game. She told me shortly before she died, "I really didn't feel well that day, but I'm glad you kept on me and took me because I had the time of my life." As a student there for seven years, I got to see all of the sporting events there, and I wanted my grandmother to experience one. I'm really glad she could do it with me. When I return there for a game in the next season, whether it's men or women, I think it'll be very emotional for me to be there and fondly recall that afternoon that my grandmother and I spent watching Kansas pound Missouri.

Julie Chappell

Julie A. Chappell, Ph.D., was born in Lawrence, Kansas, in 1950 and grew up there on her grandparents' dairy farm, the Fritzel Dairy, and at 11 E. 11th Street. She is currently an Associate Professor of British Medieval and Early Modern literature at Tarleton State University in Stephenville, Texas.

On March 26, 1952, when Clyde Lovellette was scoring 33 points against St. John's to lead KU to its first NCAA national title, I was not quite two years old. But, I was a Jayhawk and already the biggest little fan that Clyde Lovellette had.

As every Jayhawk basketball fan knows, Clyde Lovellette stands 6'9" and was a two-time All America at KU. He would become the first basketball player ever to win an NCAA title, NBA championship, and an Olympic Gold Medal. In 1952, I was not yet three feet tall. I could walk, run, and talk — accomplishments, certainly — but hardly medal-worthy.

Though my mother took me to watch Clyde play, my two-year-old psyche was too fragile for the exuberance of KU basketball in old Hoch Auditorium. That was then. But, by the time Allen Fieldhouse was dedicated in March of 1955, I had grown. In a very few years after that, I could do the Fieldhouse stomp with the best of them. KU basketball, in those days of my earliest memories, was a sensation — a thrill of bells and whistles, stomping feet, and shouts of satisfaction. My first vivid memory of Clyde Lovellette is mostly sensation, too.

In 1952, my father was a Douglas County Deputy Sheriff. He worked all the KU basketball and football games, and, at some point, he met Clyde. They became fast friends, sealed, no doubt, by Clyde's interest in police work and the gregarious nature of both young men. Of course their friendship introduced Clyde to the rest of our family, as well. It was then that the sensation of Clyde Lovellette began.

My first memory of Clyde is of the sensation of flying when he picked me up and put me on his shoulders. More than 50 years later, I couldn't say exactly where or on what day Clyde first flew me to his shoulders. But, I can say that it will be a long time before I forget that sensation of flying toward the rooftops or of the view of the world looking down from those broad shoulders. It may have been, like the Fieldhouse stomp, pretty terrifying for a small child, but I don't remember terror. Only delight in the flight.

Clyde was one of my favorite people, and I remained his loyal, little fan. He always had a smile and time to talk to that little girl he had taught to fly when he would visit in the years after he left KU. A few years after Clyde graduated, my father was elected Sheriff of Douglas County. A defining moment in my father's life certainly, but one of his proudest moments was when Clyde became a sheriff in his home county in Indiana many years later. After my father's election, Clyde became an enthusiastic visitor to "the jail."

When my father took office as Douglas County Sheriff in January 1957, we moved into the "jailhouse." The living quarters for the sheriff and his family were part of one massive, old stone building within which only a steel door separated the family quarters from the sheriff's private office, the dispatch and booking areas, and the prisoner's cells. Only steps from the jailhouse stood the county courthouse made of the same native stone. That courthouse still stands in the same place as a busy center of county government. The beautiful stone jailhouse building, sadly, has been destroyed, but the memories we made there with Clyde and with KU remain.

Surrounding this block in the 1950s were two city parks, a drugstore (including a soda fountain and a comic book rack), the Campus Hideaway (best – and first – pizza in Lawrence), an A&P, a service station (as we called them then since "full service" was the only kind of service in 1957), and a few late 19th-century sprawling Victorian houses occupied by very interesting old women who seemed happy to indulge a child's incessant curiosity about the past. And that was only one end of my new Paradise.

The full length of the main downtown street, Massachusetts Street, snaked out before me as I left the jailhouse. Along this street lay all the possible delights of a 1950s small, Midwestern city — clothing stores, shoe stores, a music store, furniture shops, Five 'n Dimes, a novelty shop with gag gifts galore and a large vat of cotton candy, and, most importantly to a country kid transplanted to town, all the movie theaters the town possessed save the two drive-ins just outside the city limits.

The four theaters originally intended to serve as "opera houses." The marbled walls in the interiors of the buildings were trimmed with local hardwoods and floored with once-expensive patterned carpets. The stage was made of the same wood and rose imposingly above the main floor seating. Painted and carved box seats for the wealthier patrons sat jealously apart from the simpler, but still stylishly appointed, balcony where the lesser folk occupied seats. By the 1930s, the doors to the élite boxes were sealed, though the boxes themselves were left intact to be admired as "art" and to lend elegance to the remaining main floor and balcony seating, which now belonged to all for enjoying the new, popular medium — film. Every Saturday afternoon over-sugared children and sibilant, blushing teens shared the theaters to watch the matinees, which gave way at night to first-run films from the major studios.

Living at 11 E. 11th Street in 1957 gave me access to all the delights of childhood that Lawrence had to offer. The greatest of these, for a seven-year-old child, would be yet another of the many contributions that KU made to my childhood in Lawrence — Saturday parades — KU Relays parades, KU Homecoming parades, KU Band Day parades. To the child I was then, it seemed as if every Saturday had a parade in it just for me. The noise of the crowd rising, the sound of the bands playing, and the KU colors flying made those days brilliant in my memory. And, inside the jailhouse, my mother had always prepared what looked like an endless, glorious spread of the best tasting food possible for the officers on duty for the parades and the athletic events they generally celebrated.

No county, city or state policeman ever went hungry on those KU Saturdays. The officers' appreciation for my mother's meals was only equaled by her joy in feeding them.

> **❝ My first memory of Clyde Lovellette is of the sensation of flying when he picked me up and put me on his shoulders. ❞**

Like Clyde Lovellette's feats on the KU basketball court just a few years before, those Saturday feasts that my mother created for the officers were legendary. Outside, Mass Street was regaled by the Crimson and Blue and a cacophony of band instruments, children's high-pitched squeals, car horns, and police sirens.

I still have a home movie that my father made of the very wet and slippery 1955 KU Relays parade. Downtown Lawrence is glorious in grey as the bands and floats move slowly down Mass Street, Crimson and Blue crepe flying damply yet keeping KU spirits high. The name of KU's own champion miler, Glenn Cunningham, comes into view splashed across the crepe of one float. It is followed on the same crepe canvas by the name of the 1955 KU miler, the great Wes Santee. My dad's fellow deputies appear on the film as they direct the flow of traffic in the parade and watch the crowd full of children bouncing from spot to spot to get a better view. People wave from windows above many of the stores that lined Mass Street in 1955, Ober's, Weaver's, Gustafson's Jewelry, and others. The newest automobiles are paraded with KU's Relays royalty, lovely young girls in less-than-flattering 1950s hairdos and clearly uncomfortable formal gowns, but all smiling bravely in the wet, cold April morning. I don't remember a Relays parade without rain but neither do I remember one without the great joy of watching the parade with a John's Novelty cotton candy in one hand and a licorice whip from Green's in the other. Ah, the glorious sugar rushes of youth.

Every parade had its "signature" feature — the Relays had the rain, Homecoming had the glamour, and Band Day had the heat. I can still remember people passing out at the halftime formation on the field in Memorial Stadium. Wool uniforms might be a comfort in 1950s Kansas winters, but they must have been nothing but torture in those hot days of Indian summer when Band Day came around. It was one thing in the cool of an autumn morning during the parade but quite another when the sun hit the field in Memorial Stadium as it always seemed to do right at halftime. Funnily enough, I never took up a band instrument.

So, in what part of my life does KU *not* figure?

My first non-family hero, Clyde Lovellette. My first college football game, Memorial Stadium. My first real sled ride, on the slippery slope of KU's Campanile Hill. My first experience of carillon bells, KU's Campanile. My first real Christmas party, the Bowersock parties in KU's Hoch Auditorium. My first (and still favorite) opera, Puccini's *Madame Butterfly*, in KU's University Theatre. My first skateboard attempt (and fall), the sidewalks on the Hill. My first attempt (and success) driving up a hill operating a stick shift *AND* coming down again unscathed, on the Hill. My first "swim" in a public fountain, KU's Chi Omega Fountain. My first job, summer catering girl at KU. My first university class, KU. My first rock concert, at Potter's Lake. My own children's first encounter with a mascot, Big Jay and Baby Jay. The first blazon on their infant tees, a Jayhawk.

What is remarkable to me is that in spite of having lived away from Lawrence for more than 20 years and holding none of my academic degrees from KU, these vivid memories from my childhood keep me inextricably bound to KU and to Lawrence. I still thrill to the sound of Rock Chalk Jayhawk, KU!

Larry Blaylock

Larry Blaylock taught in the North Kansas City School District for 29 years before retiring in 2003. He is currently a project consultant for a Kansas City remodeling company.

I must have been destined to be a Jayhawk and I have been a Jayhawk my entire life. Even though I grew up in Topeka, I was born in Lawrence. My mom graduated from KU, and my dad took me to several KU football and basketball games as a child. Ironically, my birth date falls on the same day that KU played its first basketball game and also won its 1,000th basketball game. I know I saw Wilt play, but was too young to remember it. I do remember going to basketball games in the late 1950s and being somewhat "afraid" of that big red, yellow, and blue bird that paraded around the court before games. I also remember walking out of Allen Fieldhouse in the snow after games, holding my dad's hand and noticing mostly long top coats, fedora hats, and cigarettes in many of the hands that were at my head level.

I remember sitting in the horseshoe near the field at the northwest corner of Memorial Stadium in the mid 1960s during the KU vs. Nebraska game. Gale Sayers was a senior. In the first half with the game tied 7-7, KU had the ball first and goal at the Nebraska two yard line. We ran four straight running plays and the Huskers stopped us short of the goal line each time. Late in the second half, trailing NU 14-7, KU sent Sayers on a pass route that had him running right toward where we were sitting. He had his man beat by about five yards. The pass was perfect and Sayers was about to make a beautiful over-the-shoulder catch for the game-tying touchdown. We all stood up as the ball touched Sayers' out-stretched hands only to have his knee come up and knock the ball away. We lost that game, 14-7.

As a soon to be ninth grader in the summer of 1965, I attended KU's Midwestern Music and Art Camp. It was a six-week camp and the highlight of the camp for me was playing in the pick-up basketball games on the outdoor court (it is no longer there) in the evening after dinner behind Templin Hall. There were four baskets on the court and we always had four half-court games going each night. Early one night up walks Jo Jo White and a friend. Soon we had enough players at that basket to start a game. Jo Jo wanted to play "make it, take it." I had never played that before, but soon found out what he meant. The rules were if your team made the basket, then your team got the ball back again. The only stipulation was that you had to make one pass before a team member could shoot again. That "game" became a shooting drill for Jo Jo. He started deep in one corner and worked his way around to the other corner. After each basket his friend would take the ball out of the chain net, Jo Jo would move about five feet around the perimeter to another spot and shoot again. I don't think he missed a shot and I don't think I ever touched the ball during that "game," but I didn't care. What a thrill to be on the court with one of my Jayhawk heroes!

In the mid 1990s, it was time to share what it means to be a Jayhawk with my own family. I was attending a basketball game with my wife, our two children, and another family of four. After the game, the eight of us waited outside the KU locker room hoping to get some autographs for the four kids. Coach Roy Williams walked out on his way to his post-game radio interview with Max Falkenstien. On his way back to the locker room, several autograph seekers, our four children among them, stopped Coach Williams. Our friend's two boys and my daughter were able to get his autograph. My son was one of the last ones standing along the roped off area near the door to the locker room. When Coach Williams got to my son I heard him tell my son, "I have to go in here (the locker room) for a moment. I will be right back." My nine-year-old son looked up at me, but didn't say a word. My heart sank. I was afraid Coach Williams would get busy and forget what he told my son. About five minutes passed, the door opened, and out came Roy Williams. He looked around a moment, saw my son and asked, "Are you the one I promised an autograph?" My son nodded yes and got his autograph. I was impressed!

That nine-year-old boy eventually became a student at KU. However, as a high school senior in 2006, my son was unsure about his major. One of the areas he considered was Sports Management. I called KU and set up an appointment for my son, my wife, and I to meet with someone from that department. The person we met with was Dr. Bob Fredrick (who died in 2009). I had heard about Bob Fredrick for years. What an impressive individual! We met for about 45 minutes. He made us feel so welcome and comfortable. We finished our conference and left. We had to walk about a half mile to get to where our car was parked. It was starting to rain just as we got to the door of the parking garage next to Allen Fieldhouse. We opened the door when we heard someone call my wife's name. As we turned to look back, we saw Bob Fredrick running in the rain. He was wearing his dress shoes, slacks, and a nice shirt and tie running towards us carrying my wife's purse! She had left it in his office and instead of him thinking we would notice and come back for it, this 64- to 65-year-old man ran after us! Ironically, in January 2009 we were celebrating my son's birthday at the same Lawrence restaurant where Bob Fredrick, his wife and another couple were eating. I introduced myself, re-told that story which he remembered, and told him that my son was attending KU but had decided on another major. As he left the restaurant, he stopped at our table to say hi to our group and introduced himself and his wife to our friends. At that point I understood what I had heard about Dr. Bob Fredrick. He truly was a gentleman and cared about people. My son did not take any sports management classes but did graduate from KU in 2008. What a great year that was!

Watching KU games is now a family affair for me along with my wife, my daughter, and my son. We are not always in the same room, the same city, or together at Allen or the stadium anymore, but we always communicate by text message during those games. I know most of our non-Jayhawk friends don't understand that. Only other Jayhawks understand the passion that we feel! Rock Chalk Jayhawk!

Mic Johnson

Mic Johnson enjoys reading, discussing, watching, and writing about KU basketball and football, and periodically shares his thoughts on his blog, Jaytalkers.com. Mic and his wife, Missy, met at KU. They live in Prairie Village, Kansas.

I first started following KU when my sister Marney was a freshman during the 1988 National Championship season. I've never really gotten over the fact that she got to experience that championship celebration in Lawrence instead of me. I guess that's what I get for being an annoying little brother, a role I took, and continue to take, great pride in.

My first lasting memory as a KU fan was when my dad took me to Kansas City and we participated in some of the events going on around the 1988 Final Four. For some reason (that only therapy will someday help me understand), I specifically remember watching Dick Vitale having the time of his life shooting free throws inside Crown Center. Unfortunately, we didn't have tickets to the Final Four games, so I missed out on what would undoubtedly have been my first great memory as a KU fan. Of course, I had no idea at the time how much my life would be impacted by KU in the years to come.

Before my freshman year at KU, I'd never set foot inside Allen Fieldhouse. I grew up in Wichita and was, by default, a Wichita State Shocker fan during the years of Aubrey Sherrod, Antoine Carr, Cliff Levingston, and Xavier McDaniel. After graduating from high school, I went to KU primarily because my dad "politely urged" me to as it fit into the budget and because he thought my sister Marney would look out for her younger brother. The former was accurate; the latter … not so much. But I digress …

My freshman year, 1990, was Roy Williams' second year at KU. I don't even remember who KU was playing the first time I attended a game at Allen Fieldhouse. What I do remember is that I took a girl to the game, figuring that it would impress her. We walked around the Fieldhouse for awhile, and of course we had no idea how much history oozed from every corner of that grand building. As it got closer to the start of the game, we decided to find seats. I, being a clueless freshman that had never been to a game, figured it was open seating. With my date by my side, and with me feeling like the BMOC (Big Man on Campus), I picked two seats for our Allen Fieldhouse baptism — wooden, shiny, chair backs, center court, about half-way up. Perfect! What a great spot to watch the game, I thought to myself. We sat there for a bit, enjoying the view while the Jayhawk players ran through warm-ups. A few minutes later, a couple of people came up to us and politely told us that we were in their seats. Having instantly lost my BMOC status and feeling more like a freshman than I already had, I sheepishly got up and headed down the walkway to find other seats. An older man sitting nearby saw what had happened, made eye contact with me, and as we approached him, said "Do you know whose seats you were sitting in?" to which I replied, "No." With a smile on his face and clearly not realizing that he was hurting any and all chances for me to save face with my date, he said, "Those were Phog Allen's son's seats."

And THAT was my first ever experience inside Allen Fieldhouse.

In spite of my inadequate grasp of the Allen Fieldhouse seating policy, I fell in love with KU basketball at that game and never looked back. I think Phog Allen's ghost sprinkled crimson and blue dust on me after I sat in his son's seats. He knew I wouldn't get the girl that day, so instead he gave me a love for KU basketball that knows no limits.

The season I will never forget is the 2008 National Championship. As I mentioned, I wasn't able to fully experience and appreciate the 1988 National Championship. KU went to the title game my freshman year (1990), but lost to Duke (and thus my hatred of Duke began). KU also went to the Final Four in my junior year (1993), but once again came up short.

Amazingly, I had never attended a Final Four. I didn't go in 1990 or 1993 when I was a student. When KU made it to the 2003 Final Four, I couldn't make it because my first day with a new employer was the day of the National Championship game. In hindsight, I think my heart literally would have broken had I been there when Hakim Warrick blocked Michael Lee's final shot and Carmelo Anthony cemented his "one and done" status with the Syracuse Orangemen.

> ❝ We saw Bob Fredrick running in the rain. He was wearing his dress shoes, slacks, and a nice shirt and tie running towards us carrying my wife's purse! ❞

When KU made it to the Final Four in 2008, I was determined to go to San Antonio. I had secured tickets and my wife and I were planning to make the trip along with a few friends. I can't describe how excited I was, especially knowing that Roy Williams and North Carolina were waiting for the Jayhawks. Unfortunately, all of my excitement and anticipation came to an abrupt stop. I received a call that my grandfather had passed away and the funeral ended up being the same weekend as the Final Four.

On the morning of the KU-North Carolina game, I spoke at my grandfather's funeral and we laid him to rest. That evening, several of the younger members of our family went and watched the game at a bar in Wichita. I enjoyed every second of it and I just knew that my grandfather was smiling down on all of us as we celebrated, cheered, and toasted to KU. After the final buzzer sounded, we raised our glasses in a toast to my grandfather. I knew that even though he was a lifelong Wichita State Shocker fan, Grandpa Johnson helped KU win that night.

On the night of the National Championship game, my wife, Missy, and I joined my cousin, Erica, and her husband, Dave, at Jefferson's on Massachusetts Street in Lawrence. I was glued to the television and hanging on every shot, pass, dribble, and rebound as though Bill Self would call on me to enter the game at any minute. I honestly felt like KU had a chance to win the game when they were down by nine with just over two minutes to go. I remember moving away from our table and inching closer toward the bar where I stood fixated on the game until the improbable dream unfolded right before my very eyes.

The rest of the story is history. Everyone in Jefferson's was going crazy, high-fiving, screaming, and spraying beer everywhere. Then we all ran out on to Mass St. and partied with 40,000-50,000 of our closest friends. It was the experience I had longed for during my freshman and junior years at KU and I soaked up every millisecond of it. It was pure and unfiltered joy.

I remember walking down Mass St. holding my hand in the air and gladly accepting high-five after high-five from countless fans. I remember kissing Missy and hugging her as hard as I could as I tried unsuccessfully to fight back the tears. It's difficult for me to put into words the passion I feel for KU on so many levels and it all came pouring out at that moment. The fact that my grandpa's funeral was two days earlier only added to the overwhelming emotions I was feeling. As I reflected back on that memory, I've come to believe that I wasn't supposed to be in San Antonio that weekend. I was exactly where I was meant to be and I wouldn't change a thing.

Keep Rockin' and Chalkin'!

CHAPTER 3
Becoming a Jayhawk

Calvin Thompson

From the time he started playing basketball in the sixth grade in Kansas City, Calvin Thompson knew where he wanted to attend college: the University of Kansas. Thompson did just that, helping lead the Jayhawks to the Final Four in 1986. Following a seven-year pro career, Thompson began coaching and conducting camps and clinics. In 1995, he started HOOP Service, a developmental basketball program for boys and girls in the Kansas City area.

When Larry Brown became our basketball coach in 1983, there was an immediate buzz with the fans. We lived in Jayhawk Towers and we could hear the fans outside. We realized then how big KU basketball was. After my playing days ended in 1986, I started going around and doing my Camp on Wheels in small towns across Kansas, like Eureka and Hanover, places where kids couldn't afford to go to KU, K-State, or MU camps. That was my way of saying thanks for the four years of support. That's also when I realized how crazy and wild the fans were.

There was a situation where I had gone through Marysville, Kansas, and one of my campers was named Josh Dixon. He'd call and call. He was my new best friend as a fourth-grader. He kept calling and calling to invite me to dinner and he was going to ask his friends to come over. I was going up there to do a camp, so I figured I'd go to Josh's house for dinner and get acquainted with the people. However, there was a really bad thunderstorm, and I didn't make the trip. I didn't think to call because I was just going up there to make an impromptu visit. When I got up there a few days later, this kid's step-dad sat me down in his office and he balled his eyes out. He said, "My kid hasn't slept for three days. He was so worried about you because he thought you were in an accident. You told him you were coming and you didn't show up. You don't understand, we bleed KU blue." Holy smokes! That was one of my first really big experiences after my playing days of seeing what KU fans were like.

My introduction to KU athletics came around the sixth grade in Kansas City. All I heard about was the Jayhawks. Jayhawk this and Jayhawk that. My friends at the time weren't even big KU fans. They were more NBA fans (the Kings were in Kansas City at the time). They gave me the nickname Nate Thurmond. But that was right around 1975-76, a year or two after KU went to a Final Four. I told my mom one day that I wanted to get good enough to play basketball at the University of Kansas. When I told her that, she laughed at me. That was my motivation to get better because I took that as her saying I couldn't do it. I had no idea what a scholarship was and I had never played on a basketball team, but I wanted to go to KU. Really, though, I mainly wanted to fit in with my friends.

> " My kid hasn't slept for three days. He was so worried about you because he thought you were in an accident. You told him you were coming and you didn't show up. You don't understand, we bleed KU blue. "

As a young kid back then, I was as wide as I was tall. I could shoot the ball, but I was lazy. So, I had to get creative. I would rig the net so it could come back to me. That's how I became a good shooter. I wasn't running after it, but I could shoot it. Later, I understood what hard work could do. I never took a day off, regardless of the weather. I did not take a day off and it paid off. I figured everybody wanted to score because you have to score to win. So, I learned to score and that's why I got picked to play on teams. As I got older, eighth or ninth grade, I learned the importance of running more and I started going to camps. Coach Ted Owens, Coach Bob Hill, and Jo Jo White were watching me and sending letters. Everybody knew I was going to KU.

As it worked out, I was part of Ted's last recruiting class. It was ironic because he started at KU in 1964, the year I was born. People say it wasn't electric around the basketball program because of wins and losses. My freshman year, we had three freshmen starting. We were going to be good. We were putting Kansas basketball back on the map. But they fired Ted and brought in Larry Brown.

It took awhile to buy into what Coach Brown was doing. He told us we'd be really good when, he said, he got his kids in there. I was offended as an 18-year-old freshman. It was tough to swallow because we were there. I understand that now as an adult, but it was harsh to come in there and say to a bunch of freshmen.

But he was used to dealing with grown men at the professional level. He had been a college coach, but his most recent experience was in the pros. We weren't men. We got offended and we were hurt by what he said. Things didn't click until we were all on the same page early in my junior year.

A lot of people say that excitement in the basketball program was down during Ted Owens' last couple of years. That's not entirely true. But when Coach Brown got there, they definitely became louder and more vocal. When we'd hit free throws and hear "Woooosh!" That was loud! They have always been vocal, but the thing I admire about Kansas — and I hear this from Missouri people, K-State people, and Oklahoma people — is that our fans have always been classy. They might chant something occasionally. But you never hear about an opponent getting smacked in the head with a chicken in Lawrence. Or you don't hear about fans like Missouri's Antlers. My father died during my first game at Allen Fieldhouse in my freshman year. We went to Missouri about three months later and the Antlers were yelling things at me like, "Hey, Calvin, where's your dad?" Unbelievable. But that's Missouri.

There's no place like home. And there's no place like Allen Fieldhouse. It's incredible. We could hear from the Jayhawk Towers when fans started lining up outside the night before a game. They'd start chanting, and so we'd go out and visit with them. We'd take doughnuts or pizzas. Their support was unbelievable. We had a crew that would follow us wherever we went. Coach Brown was shocked, I think, at the outpouring of support. He made sure to take care of them. They were true fans. We didn't have to go out and warm up. We were already sweaty and warm and ready to go when we heard the fans.

We were the group that started the annual tradition of "Late Night." We didn't know what to expect. To have so many fans fill up the gym at midnight — wow! We knew that Kansas was a special place. It was an unbelievable privilege to play in front of the KU fans at Allen Fieldhouse. I'm a Jayhawk for life.

Charlie Hughes

Charlie Hughes can admit it today: As a youngster, before he knew any better, he attended some football games at (gulp) Kansas State and might've even pulled for the Wildcats a little. But, thanks to a K-State football coach, Hughes became a Jayhawk fan during high school. Today, a season-ticket holder to KU football games, Hughes works in Overland Park, Kansas, as a State Farm Insurance agent.

He and his wife, Susie, have a daughter, son-in-law and grandson ... all Jayhawks.

I remember the day I became a Jayhawk fan. It was in 1969. But, the driving force began the year before.

In May 1968, I was a junior in high school. That year, we began having a sports banquet with a special guest speaker. The guest speaker that first year was Kansas State football Coach Vince Gibson. As a football player, I was curious to hear what Gibson had to say, although he wasn't recruiting me. Shoot, I wasn't big enough or fast enough to play football in college. My high school coach, Jack Dancer, played at Coffeyville and he told me that if I could live without it, to not play. I could and so I didn't.

That spring day during my junior year sports banquet, I listened to Vince Gibson talk about "Purple Pride" and "We Gonna Win." He talked a lot about himself and how he was going to turn the purple program around. I wasn't impressed, but I did attend a few K-State games that fall, mostly because my buddies were all K-State fans. And, frankly, up to that point I had gone to K-State for games more than I did at KU because more of the people in my hometown of Garnett were Kansas State fans. Besides, there were more opportunities to attend games in Manhattan. That was at a time when you could run out to your car between plays to grab a cola.

Fast forward to May 1969, my senior year. I once again attended our annual sports banquet. The speaker this time was Kansas football Coach Pepper Rogers. What a character he was, which we knew already. After all, I'll never forget the somersault he'd do as he led the Jayhawks onto the field. Speaking to our group, Rogers cracked a few jokes and talked a little about the program. Even though, with the likes of John Riggins and John Zook, he could've talked a lot about the Jayhawks, he kept that part relatively short. He then asked each senior football player to stand up one by one. He had a story about each one of us. Come to find out, he had visited with our coach prior to speaking and had come up with something to say about each one of us individually. Some of it was true, some he made up. Regardless, it made all of us feel special. I know at the age of 17, I was very impressed!

I remember one of my first times to visit Memorial Stadium. High school coaches could get passes to the games, so I went with one of my coaches. Since the stadium is just bleachers, we bought seat backs. Well, we didn't need them. We climbed to the 65th row, which was the highest in the stadium. The top wall served as our seat back. For the past several years, we've had season tickets to the football games. I sure could use that seat back now.

Our football experience hasn't been limited to Memorial Stadium, though. At the end of the 2007 football season, six of us traveled to south Florida and met up with some other people to watch the Jayhawks play Virginia Tech in the Orange Bowl, which was a huge highlight. We sat in the end zone right next to the band. If you were watching the game on TV, do you remember seeing that monstrous Mark Mangino head near the band? That was Paul Barrett, one of the guys in our group. We flew to Miami via Chicago. We paraded through the Chicago airport with that giant head and caused all sorts of commotion. Then, at a bar before the game, I stuck the stick of the Mangino head down my shirt so it looked like Mangino's face on my body. I probably posed for 200 pictures. That's nothing compared to Paul. Because he was being asked to pose for so many pictures during the game, Paul was busy and probably didn't see much of the Jayhawks' victory.

As KU fans, we're really lucky to have Mark Mangino and Bill Self as the football and basketball coaches, respectively. Obviously they've done great things for the athletic program, but they're also good with the fans. A few years ago, Bill Self was the guest speaker at a State Farm meeting in the Ozarks. The night before he spoke, he was hanging out in the hotel restaurant and talking with some State Farm people. I ran down there and introduced myself, had a photo taken with him, and told him I was a football season-ticket holder. He asked me where our seats are. I said, "Not as good as yours. We're across the stadium down a few yards and higher, section 2A, row 25, seats 5 and 6." We talked for a few more minutes and then I headed back to my room.

The next morning, Coach Self talked to our group and then took questions. Our manager, Fred Fulks, set me up as a plant to ask coach a question. When I stood up to ask mine, he got a grin on his face and said, "You're the one complaining about your football seats!" It was funny and typical Bill Self. It would be easy to see how a kid on a fence about his fandom could hear Bill Self speak at a sports banquet and instantly fall in love with the Jayhawks.

The sports banquet at Garnett continued each spring with various coaches and athletes. One year, for instance, Royals Hall of Fame pitcher Steve Busby was the guest. After high school, I ended up going to what's now Emporia State for school. My parents were both from Emporia, and Dad had graduated from the school. Still, that didn't change my own love for KU and the Jayhawks. And I owe it to the day I heard Pepper Rogers speak at our sports banquet. That was the day I became a true Jayhawk fan.

Bob Holtzman

Bob Holtzman is a reporter for ESPN, handling stories for everything from SportsCenter, to Outside the Lines. Prior to joining ESPN in 2000, Holtzman worked as a news reporter at WCPO-TV in Cincinnati. Holtzman is a 1993 graduate of KU's School of Journalism. He lives in Cincinnati with his wife and three daughters ... and he says he doesn't get back to Lawrence nearly enough.

Bob Holtzman
Photo courtesy of Rich
Arden/ESPN

For several years, my dad was the station manager at the CBS affiliate in San Diego. I started my college career at UC-Davis, but decided during my freshman year that it wasn't what I was looking for in a college. So, I started looking around. Ex-San Diego Chargers player Hank Bauer was a sportscaster where Dad worked. Hank decided to go to Kansas City to do a feature story on one of his old teammates, John Jefferson, a big star wide receiver with the Chargers who, at the time, was an assistant coach at Kansas. So, Dad decided to tag along with Hank and I decided to tag along with Dad. After all, KU was one of the handfuls of schools I was considering.

We went in October 1990. The second I stepped onto the campus, I knew that was it. It was the picture I had in my mind of what college should be. I wanted a college town with big-time sports and changing seasons ... all of those things we didn't have in San Diego. Lawrence and KU were it.

As odd as it may sound, the perfect symbol to me was a tree that was right outside Memorial Stadium, before they closed the south end. This tree was huge. And, when we visited, it was beautiful. I'd never seen a tree like this in San

Diego, simply because we didn't have the change of seasons there. I was blown away by the beauty of the campus, and that one tree was symbolic of it. It didn't hurt that the university has a great journalism school, and that's what I was going to study. The situation was just about perfect. I started there in January 1991.

Even my dad gave it a thumbs-up. And, at the time, that's saying a lot. Both of my parents were Missouri graduates. My dad, especially, was a huge MU fan. I even remember watching, in the early 1980s, Missouri in the NCAA tournament. What's funny — and he probably wouldn't admit this to his old friends — is that he told me that weekend how much nicer Lawrence was (and is) than Columbia, and how much more scenic. He didn't discourage me in the slightest. In fact, I think he encouraged me because he thought much more about Lawrence than he did Columbia.

People from both coasts figure that Kansas is totally flat and an entire state of wheat. They don't expect to see what I saw, which was a beautiful campus. More friends of mine couldn't believe I was going to KU, but even guys in Lawrence couldn't believe it, that I'd go from San Diego to Lawrence. People looked at me funny in the dorm when they found out I moved from San Diego. There's this image of southern California that's up on a pedestal. People in both places were very surprised by the move.

Coach Snyder is only dressing six players for the Wildcats' next game. The rest of the team will get dressed by themselves.

Before going to KU, being a sports fan, I knew about the basketball team and the tradition but I didn't know about the fans and the "Rock Chalk" chant. There was a bunch of eye-opening stuff that I didn't expect. Within the first few months of becoming a student there, the basketball team went to the 1991 Final Four. That was nuts because they beat Arkansas and Indiana. Then, 1992 stuck with me even more because they lost in the second round to UTEP. I remember being at Allen Fieldhouse when the buses came back with the team. There were 3,000 or so people out there, welcoming the team home after they lost. I thought, "Wow, I must've picked the right place."

That reminds me of my first game at Allen Fieldhouse, which was about three days after I arrived on campus in January 1991. I went by myself to the Missouri game that was on either a Saturday or Sunday afternoon. I had shown up on campus not knowing anyone. I had tickets to the game, so I went. I wasn't going to miss that opportunity. I sat up pretty high in one of the corners in bleachers. And I loved it! Looking back, it's strange to say I went by myself, but I did.

I'm not sure if I had ever thought through what I was expecting Allen Fieldhouse to be like. But I'll put it this way: I didn't mind being by myself for the first time. There isn't much I can equate that experience to. In 1984, the Padres went to the World Series. I would say that the excitement in San Diego when they went to the World Series was similar to any old Kansas home game. It really is that electric. That's probably the only thing I'd experienced at the time before a KU basketball game that could rival the excitement. Granted, it was against Missouri, but it was a January regular-season game. It was every bit as exciting and electric as a World Series game. That's the only type of comparison I can make.

It further reaffirmed that I picked the right place.

Dave Holtzman

Born and raised in San Diego, Dave Holtzman followed in his brother Bob's footsteps and headed for KU. What has followed is a 19-year (and counting) Crimson and Blue love affair for not only David, but also his parents (who you'll read about in a minute).

I could pretty much nail down the date of when it happened, although it happened over the course of a few days in March and April 1991. That was when KU went to the Final Four after upsetting Indiana and Arkansas, and then beat North Carolina in the semifinals. That was it for me. I was converted. I was a KU fan living in San Diego. I was 13 years old. As you probably know, once you get there, you're never the same.

Before that, I wasn't really a fan of a particular school. The closest would've been San Diego State football.

By that time, though, my oldest brother, Bob, had transferred from UC-Davis to Kansas. Once he got here, I visited him several times and fell in love with everything about it — the campus, the people, the atmosphere.

One of the first times I visited him was in October 1991 on Homecoming weekend. We went to a football game that day and then an exhibition basketball game at Allen Fieldhouse that night. The football team beat Iowa State, and then the basketball team played Athletes In Action. Bob's buddies camped out so they could get pretty good seats for us at the Fieldhouse. It was fantastic!

As you might've read in his story in this book, the funny part of Bob and I coming to Kansas was that both of our parents grew up in St. Louis and went to the University of Missouri. But, the first few minutes of them visiting my brother at KU, walking the campus, and going to their first football and basketball games in Lawrence, they were converted. They realize which school is better. My uncle is a huge Missouri guy still, so my dad and my uncle get into great arguments over KU and Missouri. My uncle doesn't understand my dad's conversion.

My parents even bought the "KU Dad" and "KU Mom" sweatshirts. Today, they're huge KU fans. At least a couple times they've gone with me to see MU play KU in Lawrence and they're always decked out in their KU stuff, cheering as loudly as anyone for the Jayhawks.

I didn't realize how passionate KU fans are until my senior year of high school. I knew it was huge in Lawrence, the state of Kansas, and the Kansas City area, but I didn't see it firsthand until the KU basketball team was playing a game in San Diego against the University of San Diego. They played in the San Diego Sports Arena, which seated 13,000 or so. Half of them were KU fans. That was bizarre to me because it was a home game for USD.

That year, although I loved KU, I also thought I wanted to go to North Carolina. But UNC, after stringing me out on several wait lists, pushed me in the right direction by not admitting me in June 1996. Imagine me a UNC fan now? I still would have been a huge KU guy no matter what.

Also during my senior year of high school, the Jayhawks beat UCLA in the Aloha Bowl, 51-30, on Christmas Day. When I went to Kansas the following fall, the Jayhawk football team was ranked in the Top 25. Of course, I was bragging to all of my friends, especially those who went to UCLA, because they kept saying I was going to "just a basketball school." Now, I could proudly reply, "We're ranked in the Top 25 in football!" Hey, I was a freshman. Well, that was the last time I was able to say that during my student career of

1996-2000. Around the third week of the season, the team was ranked No. 20 when it lost to Utah, beat Oklahoma in Norman, but then went 1-7 the rest of the year. Coach Glen Mason left after that season and was replaced by Terry Allen. Their next winning season wasn't until 2005 under Mark Mangino.

Since I've been a KU fan in the Lawrence/Kansas City area, I've seen some terrific football and basketball games. I didn't think it could get much more exciting than KU's overtime win against Georgia Tech on New Year's Day, 2005. That is, until 2008.

Not much at this point tops that season which culminated with the basketball National Championship in San Antonio. I drove to Lawrence from the Kansas City area and watched the game at a friend's house because I wanted to be in town in case KU won. I thought I was going to go home crying since KU was down by nine late in the game. But, sure enough, we ran down to Massachusetts Street after the game and tried to survive that sardine feeling. It was just a mass of people.

Luckily, my wife, who's from Topeka, is a big fan. Our first date was on January 24, 1998. The day of our first date was the KU-Texas Tech game at Allen Fieldhouse. That was Raef LaFrentz's first game back and KU beat Tech 88-49. We sat together during the game and my future wife caught a T-shirt from Roy Williams. Only time ever. Then we went on our first date that night. (Keep that opponent in mind for a minute.)

Nearly six years later, on the night of October 18, 2003, we got married. That day, KU hosted Baylor for Homecoming. So, my dad, my best friend, my brothers, and a few other people went to the Baylor game until we had to leave in the third quarter to get ready for the wedding. Four years later, when KU was hosting Baylor again, the actual date that they played, was my first son's due date. He wasn't born until a week later, but I thought it was pretty cool — if not bizarre — that his due date, our wedding anniversary, fell on the same day that Baylor was at KU again.

And, going back to that Texas Tech game. We're pretty sure that our son was conceived on the same day as the 2007 KU-Texas Tech game.

Looking back, there are several tiny reasons I came to KU. I did, I loved it, and I'm living here. It's one of the greatest decisions I've ever made.

Rock Chalk, Jayhawk!

Miles Schnaer

Miles Schnaer, a Kansas City native and Pittsburg State grad, is the owner of Crown Automotive in Lawrence. Active with various charitable endeavors, Schnaer is the founding director of Bill Self's Assists Foundation and he helped start the Crown Casting Club, which provides its 200-plus members (children and their families) the opportunity to participate in weekend fishing competitions, club meetings, seminars, and other outdoor activities each March through October.

If you're in business in Lawrence and you're not involved with KU or the athletic department, you're missing a great opportunity. An opportunity to be helping the university, but more importantly, an opportunity to be working with some wonderful people. The attitude in the athletic department isn't, "You need to do this because we're the University of Kansas." They'll say, "What can we do to help grow your

Mario Chalmers' tying three point shot in the 2008 NCAA tournament thriller.
Photo courtesy of Jeff Jacobsen/Kansas Athletics

business and what can you do to help our athletic department." They see it very much as a two-way street. Because of that relationship — and the fact that I've been driving a Corvette every summer to help cope with a midlife crisis for the past 30 years — I was asked if I wanted to furnish and drive a car in the 2008 parade celebrating the Jayhawks National Championship win over Memphis.

It sounded like it would be a lot of fun, especially if I could drive someone I know, like Danny Manning. Instead, they arranged for me to drive Mario Chalmers. I didn't know Mario at all. I had met him, but I was just a fan. When they

Mario Chalmers, riding with Miles Schnaer during the parade celebrating the 2008 national championship.
Photo courtesy of Jeff Jacobsen/Kansas Athletics

said he'd be the one, I thought, "Golly, here's this great kid. It'll be fun to get to know him a little better." Of course, I was excited also because of "the shot."

Before the parade, everyone involved went to a garage near downtown to get organized. It was self-contained, so fans weren't in there. It was a lot of fun, though, because people were taking pictures with each other and with the National Championship trophy, and getting paired with their car and driver.

> ❝ Adults were handing their babies over so Mario could touch them. ❞

We got the parade started, and when we came out of the tunnel and into downtown, it was just mobs of people. I had envisioned people watching the parade from afar. No, it was wall-to-wall people. It was so bad that I would feel a bump as I drove and then hear someone yell. I was running over people's feet! I kept yelling for people to get back; a policeman behind the car was telling people to get back. The police were great, but it was so crowded that people really didn't have anywhere to go. The Corvette was a stick shift, and I barely let the clutch out at all. I tend to get claustrophobic, so this crowd wasn't helping. I thought we'd never get to Allen Fieldhouse.

I looked back every few minutes to make sure Mario was OK. He had a glazed look like he was overwhelmed. It was hard to believe that people cared this much. The lucky ones on the front row — well, lucky, I guess, if I wasn't running over their feet — were high-fiving the players and coaches. Adults were handing their babies over so Mario could touch them. And there were piercing screams of these young girls cheering for Mario. It was quite a surreal scene. Once we got out of downtown and almost to 15th Street, the crowds lightened up. The good news is that we made it to the Fieldhouse … and there was no damage to the car.

Being able to be part of that was unbelievable. I never thought I'd be in that type of setting or situation. It was a chance of a lifetime that I may never have again. I was like a kid.

Even though I'm from the Kansas City area originally, I followed KU, but from a distance because I was so busy building my career. Before Lawrence, I was in Decatur, Illinois, and I supported the Illini, but nothing close to what I do here. When I moved to Lawrence, I knew I needed to get involved with Kansas athletics. It's been a wonderful experience.

After the KU football team won the Fort Worth Bowl in 2005, Coach Mark Mangino asked John Reagan, one of the assistant coaches, to call me and ask my ring size. John wouldn't tell me why, but several months later he came by and handed me a Fort Worth Bowl ring with my name on it. That gave me the chills. I had something similar happen at Illinois after the Illini won the Big 10 Conference championship in 1984. To be included in that level of acknowledgement was overwhelming, especially at a place like Kansas. There's a lot to be said about that. Then, after the basketball team won the National Championship, Bill Self gave me a ring and my wife a pendant. This means a lot to me personally, but it also shows how much they value people's relationships. I learned a long time ago from my parents that in life if you do the right things, you'll be rewarded but you don't know it'll come. It makes you feel good. I never tell anybody that I earned that; it was a gift from people I've gotten to know.

Even the athletes at KU are instructed to treat people right. They don't know who I am, but they're courteous kids. They're 18-22 years old and placed on pedestals by people they'll never meet, but they respect a 60-year-old guy like me.

That type of attitude comes from the top with Lew Perkins. I've gotten to know Lew since he's been at Kansas, and he's a funny, success-driven person who loves to interact with other people. I've really enjoyed getting to know him these last several years. Likewise with the people on his staff — they are very much the same way. There is no doubt in my mind that Lew and his staff have this athletic department poised for success for many years.

Another genuinely nice guy is Bill Self. What can I say — Bill is Bill. What you see is what you get. He likes to be around people and it shows by the way he treats people. He's just nice. He has his priorities right, starting with his family. He's a great family man. I've played golf with him and had dinner with him. Sitting in that type of setting, I'll look around and think how many people would love to be sitting right here. I could ramble on and on about the kind of guy he is.

About four years ago, he called me and asked if I'd visit with him in his office. We set up a time and when I went up there, he started telling me that he and Cindy wanted to start a foundation to help kids. He went through the gamut from his story, to how kids today are busy playing on computers or their video games, to how kids in the Lawrence area don't have a lot of sports facilities, to how he wants to help underprivileged kids. Then, the discussion went from a facilities issue to dealing with kids' wellness and trying to get them out and active. Thirty minutes ended up being a couple hours. I told him that any time he needed help, I'd be happy to. I'm not the best at these types of things and there are plenty of people — I'm assuming — in his life who have more experience with foundations, but he felt comfortable enough to ask me. He then asked me to be on his board. It made the hair rise up on the back of my neck that he'd think enough of me to do that. That was the start of the Assists Foundation. I'm not sure how long he and Cindy had been thinking about it. But here's a guy who has his priorities set with his family and the people around him, including the Lawrence community.

If you're around long enough, you cross paths with all kinds of people. There are people who don't really care about you, those who care about you only because of what you can do for them, and then the ones who truly care. I feel that if anything ever happened down the road, we'd be able to call each other for help. He has a lot of people around him like that. A business partner told me one time, "You'll make a lot of acquaintances during your life, but just a handful of friends. If you have a handful of friends, you're probably a pretty good guy." Bill has more than a handful of friends.

Miles and Max.
Photo courtesy of Miles Schnaer

When talking about great Jayhawks, though, I have to include Max Falkenstien. I think my favorite Max story is Max himself. He can remember things from years ago that happened and the situation whether he was broadcasting or walking downtown and ran into somebody. I experienced that first-hand with Max during the 2008 Final Four in San Antonio. I chartered a twin-engine private jet and flew Max and Randy Habiger, my Toyota Sales Manager, down to San Antonio. That weekend was unbelievable! I stayed by Max's side the entire trip, escorting him around the city — we were like two fraternity brothers for a few days. It was amazing to be walking down the River Walk and hearing all of these people yell, "Hey, Max!" Seemingly every KU fan wanted to say something to him. The funny thing is that Max doesn't see himself as an icon at KU. But he is. That entire weekend — being with Max and watching the Jayhawks win the National Championship — is easily one of the most overwhelming experiences in my life.

There's nobody I'd rather have as a spokesperson for my business than Max. He respects people around him. He's still involved with the athletic department and people around there love him. Max is an icon, no doubt about it. When I have lunch with him and we're talking about life, I tell him that he doesn't know how many of my friends and KU supporters would die — or at least pay good money — to be sitting there with Max, soaking in his stories. Who wouldn't want to sit and talk with Max? For a guy who loves people, that's the best.

Bill and Max are great examples that the people with KU are inclusive. They appreciate what supporters do for the success of the program. You don't feel like they expect you to do things because they're KU. I'm living an out-of-body experience in my life and my career and the things I've been involved with. KU athletics is at the top of that list.

Chris Simkulet

Chris Simkulet, who recently purchased her first home in Kansas City, Kansas, is a professional liability underwriter. When she's not pulling for the Jayhawks, she enjoys watching live sporting events, from the pros down to AAU tournaments.

I was on the Hill between 1995 and 2000. I grew up in upstate New York and came to KU because I fell in love with the basketball program — the crush on Steve Woodberry didn't hurt, either! Frankly, I grew up a Syracuse fan (blasphemy, I know!). As you probably know, ESPN's "Big Monday" has always had a Big East game followed by the Big 8 (now Big 12) game. In the early 1990s, TV ratings meant that it was usually a Syracuse game followed by a KU game. The rest is history. I just fell in love with the style of basketball and the program and traditions at KU. And again, the crush on Woodberry didn't hurt! At the time I was going to double major in astronomy and archeology — don't ask, I don't know why. Anyway, not many schools offered both as majors, but KU did. Getting to move halfway across the country from my parents was just an added bonus (I was a bit of a rebel child). Fortunately for me, out-of-state tuition at KU and in-state tuition at any of the SUNY (state university of New York) schools were actually quite comparable. So, other than the added travel expense, it was basically a wash and that's how I finally convinced my parents to let me come to the Midwest. I would have to say, then, that I've been a true fan since about 1993 — but I do still have the 1991 Final Four on VHS, too. After the 1993 Final Four, though, that was it. I was hooked. No questions asked. From that point on it was just trying to figure out how to make it happen.

When I arrived at KU, I did pull a total "freshman" the first time I walked inside the Fieldhouse — and, of course, Steve Woodberry was there. It was August of my freshman year and I had NO idea about anything, let alone that you might be able to just walk into the Fieldhouse, but a friend of mine took me over there. When I walked in the southeast tunnel to the court, I stood there, jaw dropped, and did a 360-degree spin that felt like it lasted 30 minutes! I'm sure I looked like a total fool to anyone who saw me, but it was my honest-to-goodness reaction! I never visited campus before I came out for orientation that August, so it was the first time I'd seen anything like the Fieldhouse in person. After I composed myself, we walked over to the north bleachers to watch some guys playing pick-up basketball and Woodberry was sitting there. I felt like a complete moron because there's no telling how it looked to him to see this new girl on campus spinning around inside the Fieldhouse. It's all good, though. At least he knew I was a Jayhawk! (I never did get to actually meet him, though.)

Over time, because I lived in Jayhawk Towers my junior year, I became pretty good friends with some of the guys. Paul Pierce and I used to hang out quite a bit. I worked at Kmart at the time and he and I went over there one day to get some stuff, and I remember all of my co-workers following him around the store and just being baffled that I knew Paul Pierce! That was funny — to me, he was just a regular guy (who happened to be really good at basketball)! Travis Williams (a medical redshirt in 1994-95 who never actually got to play because of his back) and I are really good friends still. He was a local Kansas boy that Roy Williams recruited. He is 7'2", so too bad his back was never diagnosed correctly back then!

Even though I've been a fan for only about 15 years, I don't remember the very first KU game I watched. But I do remember wearing my Jayhawk shirts to the Carrier Dome when I would go to Syracuse games. My uncle has season tickets still (maybe 30 years now) and every time I go, I'm wearing Jayhawks all over! I did get to see Roy Williams' North Carolina team win the Regionals there in 2005. That's bittersweet, though. That leads me to my most disappointing time as a fan; when Roy left. I'm not mad that he left, and I understand why he left, but I don't understand why he lied to us a couple years before that. He promised each and every Jayhawk fan that he would never leave that day when the phrase "I'm staying" came out of his mouth. Jayhawks took that to heart and took it as a personal insult when he went back on his word — at least I did. I was one of the approximately 16,300 fans at Memorial Stadium when he made that promise. A promise that he broke. He had a chance at making his own legacy at KU, but instead he chose to forever walk in shadows at his alma mater. What still gets me, though, is that KU is Dean Smith's alma mater. One other disappointing moment was our loss to Arizona in the NCAA Tournament in 1997. We just didn't play like a team — and in talking to some of the guys later, I guess they all felt it, too, but no one said anything and stood up to fix it. That's just one of those life lessons they all learned that day, but we all paid for.

During my junior year, in 1998, I won "fan of the game" for the Iowa State game. I was all dressed up with pom-pons for a skirt, and painted up red and blue. But the topper was the mini-hoop (I stuck hooks in a baseball cap that I wore backwards so a basketball net was covering my face.) When we went out to center court (me and the 12-year-old kid I was competing against), the kid started "beating up" his Cyclone doll. I didn't even plan on having a gimmick! So I just took the ball that went with the mini-hoop that I had been squeezing out of stage fright and tossed it as high I could ... and caught it in the hoop! TWICE! It sure is a great feeling to have 16,300 people cheering for you! That's something I can say that I now share with some of the greatest basketball players to ever walk the planet.

But my favorite moment at KU is a day I will never forget. It was Saturday, January 17, 1998, the day Wilt Chamberlain returned to have his jersey retired. I'm tearing up with joy and sadness as I talk about it now. He stood in the tunnel, a GIANT of a man. And it wasn't just his height. It was his overall physical size, and the size of his personality that was just beaming out of him. He was more than just an amazing basketball player, an amazing athlete, or amazing business man — he was an amazing human

> How do you get a
> K-State fan off
> your porch?
>
> Pay him for the
> pizza.

being. He wanted to excel at everything he did. And he achieved that. That day in 1998, I witnessed him excel at being a Jayhawk. Who can blame him thinking for all those years that we might hold it against him for not winning in triple overtime (in the National Championship game against North Carolina in 1957)? That's just proof he was a competitor. Favorite all time player — Wilt. Met him that day when I got his autograph. I asked him to put his number, too, and he laughed and asked if I wanted the autograph or the number — and I said both! He was just a quick-witted, admirable person and someone I've always looked up to — and always will. But I am so glad for his soul — and for mine — that he found it within himself to accept his place on the walls of the greatest basketball arena in the world. Only a Jayhawk would think that they might not be good enough to be a Jayhawk. But he was. In my opinion, he was the greatest Jayhawk of all time.

As far as a favorite season, I would have to say the 100-year anniversary season. Of course, I wasn't too disappointed with the 2007-08 season, either! My parents had been to Kansas only to drop me off in 1995, for graduation in 2000, and then for the victory parade. They happened to be coming out just to visit me in Kansas City last year. They landed on Saturday, so we went to Lawrence on Sunday! They had a blast! My dad is a golfer (former pro, turned retired history teacher) and my mom is more interested in Saratoga (but still a librarian), and even though they have never quite grasped my connection with KU, they understand that it exists and they were able to share that with me that day. That was pretty special. Of course, my dad being a New Yorker, he pushed his way to the front of the pack to get some great pictures of the guys as they came down Massachusetts Street! Gotta love it!

Even though I came to the Midwest from upstate New York, I was adopted as a baby, so I have no doubt in my mind that I was born to be a Jayhawk. It just took a couple years to figure that out! But considering where I grew up, I'm just glad I eventually did! It's in my blood. I can't explain that, but other Jayhawks know exactly what I mean.

CHAPTER 4
Jayhawks Are Everywhere!

Sadie Windego

Sadie Windego is a teacher in Fort Frances, Ontario, Canada, by way of Paola, Kansas. She graduated from the University of Kansas in 2000, with a major in middle/ secondary social studies education and a minor in special education. She taught for five years in Kansas and Texas, before moving to Ontario, where she's spreading her love of the Jayhawks.

I have always been an emotional and intense Kansas fan. My entire family has a love and passion for the Jayhawks that is hard to match. My love for the Jayhawks is extreme and endless. It has always been and will always be.

My dad might be one of the greatest fans of all time, and I learned my passion from him. When the games were on — football or basketball — and the windows were open, the entire neighborhood could hear him cheering. I have the same enthusiasm and love for Kansas that he does. He is a KU alum, along with my grandfather and other family members. When a game is on, our house is very loud, filled with cheering and yelling. When we were young, my dad would take us to Lawrence. He would talk about KU with such pride and excitement. He always made it seem like it was the greatest place on earth. He told stories of old basketball and football teams and games he remembered seeing. He always told those stories with a smile.

Hands down, my favorite player is Danny Manning. He always has been and always will be. I was in fourth grade when we won the 1988 National Championship. I remember it like it was yesterday. I was allowed out of school to attend the KU parade in Lawrence after they won the championship. Every other year, when we were knocked out of the tournament, I would cry myself to sleep. But, Danny

Manning was the ultimate player in my mind. That year, 1988, was a presidential election year, and I had a sticker on my desk that said "Danny Manning for President." On my birthday, I begged my parents to invite Danny to my party. They had a Jayhawk cake made for me that said "Happy Birthday. Love ya, Danny." That was good, but I really wanted him there!

I graduated from Paola High School in 1996 and, obviously, went to KU. My most memorable game at Allen Fieldhouse was my freshman year. It was over Christmas break. I lived in Jayhawk Towers then, so they did not close at Christmas like the dorms. Some friends and I decided we were going to camp out for the Texas game. We would stay at the Towers, so we could get good student seats. We were ready for the big game with signs we had made, and seats on the very bottom row of the student section. Dick Vitale was announcing that game for ESPN, and he signed our signs. During the game, we were on TV several times, including one time that Vitale talked on the air about meeting us.

After I graduated from KU, I went to graduate school at the University of North Texas in Denton. I was in the Emotional/Behavioral Disorders Program and began doing practicum in different alternative schools and self-contained ED classrooms. I worked with students who had very severe behavioral and emotional disorders.

There were a couple great KU stories during my time there. I had a girl who had severe learning disabilities and would never talk. I worked there for a year before she would talk to me. She didn't talk to anyone. She would listen, but not talk. On my desk I always had a Jayhawk propped on the front. One day I saw this girl drawing. I just watched because I was so amazed of her hidden talent. She walked up to my desk and handed me the picture, still not saying anything. The picture was a beautiful, perfectly drawn Jayhawk. I could not believe it! It was perfect! I had found a way to communicate with her through her artistic talent. After that she opened up and finally talked to me. I asked her to draw me a poster with a big Jayhawk on it and paint it, which she did. I laminated it and it has been in every classroom I have taught in since. That was special.

During the 2007-08 school year, while waiting for my Ontario teaching license, I worked as an educational assistant. I worked at St. Francis School in the fifth and sixth grade class.

Once the 2008 NCAA men's basketball tournament started, I began wearing a KU shirt daily. Eventually, the students began asking why. I explained to them that the University of Kansas was my alma mater and that I had been a Jayhawk fan from as far back as I can remember. Once we were in the Final Four, I really began to express my excitement and talked about how amazing it was that we had made it to that level. In Canada, university athletics are not as popular as they are in the States. I had to explain what it meant to be a Jayhawk and how important this really was. I had Jayhawk stickers made and many of the students at St. Francis were wearing them the Friday before the Final Four. On that day, my sixth grade class came to school with their faces painted in crimson and blue and some even made T-shirts. The girls had created a KU cheer. This meant so much because I live in a hockey town, like most in Canada. My enthusiasm for my beloved Jayhawks had expanded and was instilled in a group of impressionable young people. I was so touched. My eyes were teary several times that day.

At the end of the day, my students were determined to get me to do the KU fight song and I certainly owed it to them.

So, at the end of the day, I sang "Cause I'm a Jayhawk." They really enjoyed that and were soon looking up the song on the Internet. The Kansas spirit had spread throughout the entire school and all the teachers, administrators, and students were talking about the Kansas Jayhawks and the possibility of them becoming the National Champions.

On the Monday of the championship game, I was at school physically, but had nothing on my mind but the game that night. I then explained to the class the history of the Jayhawk, what it is and what it means. I also told them that, in my family, it is a family tradition to attend KU. I am certain that I had convinced some of the kids that the University of Kansas is the greatest school on the face of this earth!

That night, I was completely on edge watching that game. I was yelling, screaming, crying, and cheering. The win in overtime was truly amazing. I began screaming down the street and honking the horn in our car to let everyone know of my excitement. I was so thrilled, I barely slept that night. I went to school the next morning and was greeted by an announcement congratulating the Kansas Jayhawks, Mrs. Bujold's sixth grade class, and Mrs. Windego. It was so special. The entire school began cheering. I was fully crying at this point and my pride in St. Francis School and the Kansas Jayhawks was immense.

I soon learned that most of the students' parents allowed their children to stay up late and watch the entire game. The students were definitely tired that day, and may not have paid as much attention in school as they should have, but they had learned something the night before that was truly amazing. They had learned that having pride and enthusiasm in something that means something to you will give you gratification and happiness. They also learned that hard work will help you reach your dreams, like the 2007-08 Kansas men's basketball team. They will remember that their entire lives. I know that through that experience, I taught those kids principles that they will use in their future endeavors.

Brad Myers

Oklahoma City

I'm originally from Topeka, but as a student at a small college in Oklahoma, my heart was always home when we walked into Allen Fieldhouse for a game. During four years at school out of state, I attended about 25 home games, as well as both Oklahoma State and Oklahoma games against KU that were in Stillwater and Norman. We were always ribbed for wearing KU blue to those games, and sometimes walked out with our tails between our legs, none worse than Bill Self's first year taking the Hawks to OSU ... brutal. I was at the infamous Doug Gottlieb game when we all chanted "shorts on backwards," and watched as coach Eddie Sutton huddled the team around Gottlieb to change. Many memories flood my mind while remembering the beloved Jayhawks. I have to think about Dr. Patrick Barker, who without hesitation gave us tickets so we could attend games, and who is always a great friend during tournament time. We have been lucky enough to have the Barker family down to Oklahoma City the last couple times the Big 12 has been in OKC, and will continue to do so. We sat right behind the KU bench on the floor in 2009, when Bill was not the happiest of campers, but remained cool and collected during the entire game. All I can say is Rock Chalk, Jayhawk!

Gary and Terry Wallace

KU Class of 1977, Southwest Florida Jayhawks Alumni Club

We had to write you this story about our loyal Jayhawk fans here in southwest Florida. Our regular meeting place, Nick and Stella's, could not carry the KU-Missouri game a few years ago, because the local CBS station was showing the Minnesota vs. Illinois game at 2 p.m. With that obstacle, we all gathered at our backup bar, Courtside at the Sanibel Harbour Resort. They have a very elaborate satellite system which carries over 1,000 stations. They assured us on that Saturday that they could get the CBS Midwest broadcast. We arrived at the restaurant and the manager who is an expert on their system found that CBS had blocked the transmission.

Here we were, 22 excited fans waiting to see the FINAL game of the season against our old pals the Tigers and no television viewing. We all anxiously waited for the game to come on, applying our Jayhawk stickers, and putting the Jayhawk table-tops out for the game. Finally, the manager, after much due diligence, informed us sadly that he could not get our transmission.

We all joked that we would gladly listen to it on the radio of any kind. One of our fans, Ken, got an idea where he once was able to get the updates on our games from his daughter in Olathe, Kansas, by calling her cell phone. He called her and she put her cell phone by her television. Then lo-and-behold, we were able to listen by speaker from his cell phone with the commentary from her TV broadcast. We were all pretty excited just to hear what was going on in Columbia.

Jayhawk fans in Southwest Florida listen to games on cell phones, if necessary.
Photo courtesy of Terry Wallace

During the second half, when the game clock was around 6 minutes left, our local station switched from the Minnesota and Illinois game which was a blowout to the Kansas and Missouri game. We really got the place rocking when that broadcast came on. Everyone knew that the Jayhawks were having one heck of a game. It was a real nail biter. Aaron Miles hit a three-pointer falling backwards, Kirk Hinrich hit another beautiful three, Nick Collison's fantastic rebounding, and the final free throw made it one of the most gratifying games of the season. We were one jubilant fan club.

As always, Go Jayhawks!

Michael Simpson

Michael Simpson lives in Rochester, New York. When he's not watching KU, his spare time is spent performing with the Empire Statesmen Drum and Bugle Corps.

There's something you should know about me right away. I am from Rochester, New York. I have never resided in Kansas, or been close to anyone who has. I have a tough time explaining to folks how I came to be a Kansas fan. I was shopping in Syracuse, N.Y. in the late 1990s, and I found a blue shirt that, in a very cool and unique font, stated "Rock Chalk Jayhawk." I had no idea what it meant, but I bought it. I went home and looked it up, and that is how I got my first lesson into the amazing history that is the University of Kansas.

My curiosity quickly turned into an admiration, and eventually into obsession. I went from pulling for Kansas in the tournament, and learning about the players, to following the recruiting and answering my phone whenever the Rock Chalk chant rang from my pocket.

This went on all the way until 2008. I decided it was time to make my pilgrimage to Allen Fieldhouse. I chose to come out for the Kansas State game, and hopefully watch the Jayhawks take revenge on Michael Beasley. I would make the trip by myself, and the hardest part was finding a single ticket in an environment that even Coach Bill Self described as "the hardest tickets to find" in his tenure at KU. I found a seat in section 2A, and booked my trip. I packed a suitcase, but barely. I wanted enough room for the shopping spree that would occur when I could walk into a store and see only Kansas gear. The only item I had seen in a store to that date was the same shirt mentioned earlier in this story.

I arrived at the Econolodge in Lawrence on Friday, the day before the game, and got into a discussion with the woman at the front desk. She heard my story of how and why I made this trip, and she started writing down landmarks I had to see. I called a cab, and asked to be taken somewhere I could find Jayhawk gear. The driver dropped me off on Mass Street, right across from Free State Brewery. She told me that I would find everything I needed on this street, and that my journey should end here for dinner if I wanted a meal that I could not get in New York. Two hours later, I walked into the brewery with $400 worth of jerseys, shirts, shot glasses, banners and hats, from numerous stores all within 10 minutes of where I was dropped off. I was served an incredible meal and some Irish Ale that I craved the rest of the trip.

With a long day ahead of me on Saturday, I decided to go to Borders and pick up a movie to watch in my hotel and unwind for the night. It was an uneventful purchase, until I left and a nice gentleman held the door for me. I looked up to thank none other than ESPN's Digger Phelps. He was there for a book signing before Saturday's Gameday. I wanted to go back in and get his book and thusly his autograph, but I saw my cab pull up. He told me to enjoy the game, and shook my hand.

The day of the game was here. At 7 a.m., I found my way to Allen Fieldhouse and stood in line to get in to the ESPN Gameday taping, only 10 feet from the statue of Phog Allen. It was more impressive than any image I had seen on TV. That is the last time I will use that phrase — "more impressive" — in this story, but it is not the last time it is deserved. When the doors opened promptly at 8 a.m., people flooded into the arena and tried to get the best seats behind the desk where the Gameday crew would sit. I was close to the front of the line, so I would have been able to get prime seating. One problem, once inside the doors, I had no idea where I was going. I eventually found a seat in the last row of the first level. Within the next five minutes, I experienced something that would diminish any game I ever watched on TV again. I participated in my first ever Rock Chalk chant. (At least my first where others participated as well.) The goose bumps I felt then are matched only by the ones I feel right now, retelling this event.

During the taping, a few of the players happened in and took a seat on the opposite side from the fans to watch the taping. And then in a black jumpsuit, Bill Self took a seat by himself in one of the sections across from me. I left my section and walked around to the other side to try and get a picture, but was quickly deterred by a security guard who said we weren't allowed over there. I pleaded with him it was my first time here and that I was just hoping to get a picture with Coach Self. The guard wasn't having any part of it and helped turn me around and I started back toward

my seat, respectfully and without a fight, until we both looked up at a whistle we heard. And, there was the outstretched arm of Bill Self. He shook my hand and said, "Welcome to Lawrence. Thanks for coming out." I can't remember what I replied back to him, but I was numb to the point that I am sure he couldn't understand it, whatever it was.

> I ran into a Cornhusker fan the other day. Then, I backed up and ran into him again.

After the taping, I was shown around campus by a student named Josh Brosius. I remember his name, because he had mentioned to me that he was a second cousin of Scott Brosius, who played baseball for the Yankees. He helped me find my way to the campus bookstore where my next celebrity run-in would occur. I went to a book signing by Gale Sayers. He was very polite and friendly and didn't mind sharing a few words with each fan despite the growing line waiting for him.

When I eventually made it back to the Fieldhouse for the game, the biggest surprise for me was the people around me, whom I quickly befriended. They all told me their stories and listened as I told them much of what is written above. I talked with a man from Chicago who came to visit his two sons, both students at KU. Another man used his company's tickets to bring his wife and two sons to the game. We all had a blast together. They made sure I had the best view for the video playing before the Jayhawk introductions. They were shocked at how much I knew about the rituals of the game, from the shaking newspapers during the K-State player introductions, to the emphatic "New York, New York" as Russell Robinson was introduced to the crowd.

I'll admit, I was alarmed at the noise level. The game hadn't even started and you could see a young K-State team looking in the stands during the shootaround, with eyes wide enough that I could see them from the last row. A few of the Wildcats disappeared into the tunnel, only to emerge minutes later with headphones, cords hidden inside their jerseys, just trying to block out the noise. Michael Beasley was greeted with a chorus of boos, because he had told the media that K-State would beat Kansas in Lawrence, in Manhattan, or in Africa. He tried to be flashy during the pregame, but on a dunk attempt he got stuffed by the rim and fell backwards. The student section erupted in laughter.

The game went by too quickly. Soon it was halftime, and the gentleman sitting next to me told me to follow him and his sons. He took me down to a tunnel, and I walked to the edge and I was on the ground level looking up into the crowd, and I couldn't imagine trying to play a game with all of this around me, even during halftime. Before I could even take in the environment, Dick Vitale was in front of me shaking hands with the kids I had followed down with their father. We watched the team run through the tunnel back onto the court, and headed back up to our seats.

A couple had been nice enough to watch my bags of souvenirs I had purchased in the gift shop as you enter the Fieldhouse, so that I didn't have to carry them on my little side trip.

When I got back to my seat, the couple advised me to look in my bag. They had taken the time to visit the shop and pick up something for me to remember my first game. As I pulled out the piece of blue cloth sitting at the top of many other souvenirs, they explained that I deserved this shirt. I held up a shirt that on the front, in the same font as my Rock Chalk Jayhawk shirt, exclaimed "I'm a Jayhawk." This just about had me crying. I flipped it over to read "We Are Kansas." I have never been so proud to be a part of something as I felt that night.

Bill Moorhead

Bill Moorhead, who spent most of his childhood in Lawrence, is the senior pastor at Pacific Hills Lutheran Church in Omaha, Nebraska, where he lives with his wife, Martha — a Lawrence girl and a proud Jayhawk.

I was born in Waterloo, Iowa, but we moved to Lawrence in 1955, when I was 8. My parents had built a home on Greever Terrace, south of Lawrence High School and west of Centennial Elementary School. It was the same year Wilt Chamberlain came to KU as a freshman. It didn't take me long to catch Jayhawk fever. I read every *Lawrence Journal World* article and listened to every game on radio.

Bill Moorehead

Photo courtesy of Bill Moorehead

When my dad retired from the Sunflower Ammunition Plant in 1979, he was the Commander's Representative. I graduated in 1965 from Lawrence High School, which is where I met my wife, Martha. I did not attend KU — instead, I went to two Lutheran colleges to complete my degree. However, I did have the good fortune of marrying into KU, so to speak. Martha graduated from there in 1969. Her father graduated from KU in 1920. (Also, Sarah, our daughter, graduated in 1998 with a degree in psychology.)

There's actually a piece of family lore involving my wife's side of the family and the inventor of basketball, Dr. James Naismith. It involves my father-in-law, Byron Beery. Born in 1898, he was 49 when my wife Martha was born in Lawrence. Family members generally agree that Byron not only had James Naismith as a professor at some point during his college years, but also dated James Naismith's daughter, Helen, once or twice. My church league softball coach, Lew Llewellyn, presently lives at 1700 Mississippi, a home Dr. Naismith once lived in.

Regardless of that family lore, I got close to Dr. Naismith. Well, somewhat. Duke D'Ambra, a Lawrence photographer and close friend of James Naismith, is responsible for most of the pictures we see today of Dr. Naismith. Duke was well-known around Lawrence and in constant demand. I met him in June 1960, when he took our confirmation class picture at Immanuel Lutheran Church.

My wife grew up with Candy Williams, the granddaughter of Phog Allen. Martha lived at 600 Ohio. Phog, I believe, lived in the 800 block of Indiana. Martha, Candy, and the other young girls in the neighborhood used to be in and out of Phog's house all the time, especially in the summer. He was just a neighbor then, not history or legend. I have his autograph. Below his name he wrote "88 years old," so I must have gotten it shortly before he died.

In the 1950s, when our family moved to Lawrence and I became an instant Jayhawk, elementary students could be a KUFF (football) or a KUBB (basketball). For a dollar you got a big metal badge and four tickets to games. Designated group seating, of course, but what a deal! I remember how open and accessible locker rooms and players areas were in those days, especially to us kids. It seemed like we could go anywhere and not be bothered. Wilt loved all us kids and he would call us by our names. It seemed like he enjoyed nothing better than having kids flock around him. For us, nothing better than being able to call a big star like that your friend.

Access back then to the football locker room was also pretty open, at least to a young kid. I met Curtis McClinton that way and a lineman by the last name of Woodeschick, who took a special interest in me. Of course, if you were a young kid with a bicycle back then, you could watch some of these Jayhawks play American Legion baseball at the stadium on East 11th Street. I remember seeing Doyle Schick hit a home run. We also used to ride our bikes to KU to watch the Jayhawks play baseball, and maybe get a broken bat or two.

Long-time football Coach Don Fambrough, his wife Del, and their family lived in the Centennial area, so I went to school with their two sons, Preston and Bobby. Del eventually was one of my favorite teachers at Central Junior High. And what I recall about Don back then was the time he spent one summer with John Hadl, teaching him to be a quarterback when KU decided they wanted him to switch backfield positions. Since the Fambroughs lived on Alabama Street west of the high school, Don and John could be seen on many days and evenings working in the big open west meadow of the high school property.

I remember one day very early in the fall of 1959, when I was a 7th grader at Central Junior High, there was a PA announcement for anyone interested in working concessions at KU football games to come to a certain room after school to get information. When I showed up, there were two KU students there recruiting us to work. I was interested and from that point on ended up working concessions for practically every football and basketball game from 1959-1965. This was back in the day when we'd carry trays of sodas up and down the steps of the stadium and at Allen Fieldhouse. I sold sodas and eventually hot dogs, and then later I worked to keep all the concession stands running, which meant on a football day showing up at the stadium at 6 a.m. In about 1964, I worked all day for Homecoming and then worked the Harry Belafonte Homecoming Concert that night at the Fieldhouse. I got home about 2 a.m., dead tired. But I made good money that day. Harry Belafonte's road manager tipped me $20!

I recall two examples of incredible crowd noise at games. One was the KU football victory over Oklahoma in 1964, I believe, when KU scored a touchdown as time ran out, and then scored a 2-point conversion to win the game by a point. I was home listening to the game on radio and when KU won, I ran out to the back yard to tell my dad. As I ran out of the house, I could hear the fans at the stadium roaring. Our house was two miles south of the stadium.

The other was the KU-UCLA basketball game in December 1995, the game KU won by 16 after being down by 16 at the half. Somehow we managed to get tickets, but we were way up in a corner. It was incredibly loud in Allen Fieldhouse in that second half, especially when Jacque Vaughn stole the ball, drove the length of the court, and made a twisting layup to finally take the lead. I was shouting into my wife's ear and she still could not understand what I was saying. The noise literally beat on our heads!

In 1977, after working with two Lutheran churches in Kansas, a congregation in Omaha offered me a position as the youth and education pastor. (We've lived in Omaha and worked with that church, Pacific Hills Lutheran, ever since.) In the mid 1990s, Roy Williams sent me some over-sized athletic shoes for the men's shelter in Omaha. The shelter housed some men with big feet, and it was hard to find the right sizes for them. The first shipment was two large boxes full of new and used shoes of every description and size, some still in their original boxes. A couple of months later another box arrived, with a simple note: "Here's another bunch of shoes for the men. Roy Williams"

But here's the story I never tire of telling. It's 1987 and we were thinking the 1987-88 basketball team was going to be good. We knew the 1988 Final Four would be at Kemper Arena in Kansas City, so we applied for three tickets through the NCAA lottery. That was in about April. In late June, we came back to town after being gone a few days, and we had a notice in our mail of a certified delivery being held for us at the post office. We got the tickets! I put them into the bank box and started planning. Except I (a Lutheran pastor) noticed that the 1988 Final Four was going to be on

Easter weekend. So, here's how we handled it. We drove down to Kansas City on Saturday, April 2, to attend the first game. Fortunately, the KU-Duke game was the first game of the night. Then we drove back to Omaha through bad weather and the time change (we lost an hour that weekend to daylight savings time) so that I could handle Easter Sunday morning. I had yelled so loudly at the game that I could hardly chant the Easter liturgy. And all my parish members knew why. We went back down to K.C. on Monday, April 4, stayed there after KU beat Oklahoma for the national title, and then came back to Omaha on Tuesday. Our family will never forget that weekend. And, by the way, I was offered $1,575 for those tickets and declined. I even had someone still trying to get my Monday night tickets at halftime of the Saturday game.

The memories of being a Jayhawk are priceless.

Jared Projansky

Most teenagers have a tough time telling you what they're doing nine minutes from now, let alone 10 years from now. Well, Jared Projansky can tell you that nine years from now, he'll be graduating from KU. Jared, at the age of 13, submitted this story.

I was destined to be a KU basketball fan. It is in my blood. I never had a choice. Despite living in the Chicagoland area, I am all Kansas Jayhawk!

My first experience with Kansas Jayhawks basketball was on December 2, 1995. I attended the Kansas vs. UCLA game while comfortably tucked in my mother's womb. My comfort didn't last long as Allen Fieldhouse was rocking that afternoon. I was well aware that the Jayhawks came into the game ranked No. 2 in the country and defending national champion UCLA was ranked No. 23. Much to my dismay, the Jayhawks were not having a good afternoon and found themselves down at halftime. We couldn't hit a shot and the Bruins were out-rebounding us badly.

Jared Projansky

Photo courtesy of Jared Projansky

I was a little down at the half, but had confidence that the Hawks would come out stronger in the second half. While my due date was not for another four-and-a-half months, I was spot on in my prediction. The Jayhawks came out and played an outstanding second half. My dad, who attended KU from 1984-1988, said that he couldn't recall the Fieldhouse ever being louder and crazier than it was in the second half of the game. Not only did the Jayhawks win the game, but we outscored UCLA by 30 in the second half and won.

A Jayhawk is Born.

Let's get back to that due date I mentioned previously. My due date was March 17, 1996. Of course I wasn't willing to wait while my destiny with Jayhawk lore was at stake. I punched my way into the world on March 1, 1996. It was no coincidence that I picked March 1. All Jayhawk fans know that March 1 is also the birthday of Allen Fieldhouse. The Fieldhouse was dedicated on March 1, 1955. I am proud to say that I share my birthday with my favorite building. Allen Fieldhouse is my personal heaven.

So, the first KU game that I saw live and in person was on December 7, 1996. It was a rematch of the previous year's

KU-UCLA game, but this time it was at Pauley Pavilion. The Jayhawks jumped out to an early lead thanks to a couple of beautiful alley-oop dunks. As I screamed in joy some of the wine-and-cheese UCLA fans looked at me in dismay. I couldn't speak yet, but I'm sure I shot them an "I'm a Jayhawk and I am proud" look and kept cheering for the crimson and the blue. A few folks

> **❝I couldn't help myself. I had just turned 7 years old, so it is excusable that I instinctively punched my mom in the face for teasing me. ❞**

mentioned the previous season when UCLA had the big halftime lead, but I assured them that the Jayhawks were not about to let a 21-point lead evaporate. We cruised to a win and validated our No. 1 ranking.

However, I did find myself in big trouble at the age of 7 while watching KU play Syracuse in the NCAA championship game in 2003. My dad didn't take me with him to New Orleans. I had to stay home and watch the game with my mom, my sister, and my brother. Everyone loves the Jayhawks except Mom. Mom didn't like that my Dad went to so many games so she started to root against the Jayhawks. It used to make me mad, but never madder than when she was so loud in rooting for Syracuse. When Michael Lee's three-point shot was blocked to effectively end the game, Mom let out a yell. I couldn't help myself. I had just turned 7 years old, so it is excusable that I instinctively punched her in the face for teasing me. Not one of my better moments, especially looking back now. But, the best payback came 14 days later when the Jayhawks hired Bill Self away from Illinois, Mom's alma mater. I guess I got the last laugh even if I got in trouble for inexcusably hitting Mom.

Two years later, the KU Athletic Department was kind enough to throw a birthday party for me at Allen Fieldhouse.

FOR JAYHAWKS FANS ONLY!

Well, OK, the celebration was for the Fieldhouse, but when you share a passion and the same birthday, so to speak, you can take liberties like that. However, it was actually on March 2, when KU hosted the Kansas State Wildcats. While it was a special night, on the court it was business as usual as the Hawks beat the Wildcats for the 30th consecutive time. It was also my first experience with a Jayhawk Senior Night. All I can say is "Wow!" Sure, I was only 9 years old, but I made my dad stay for every second of the senior night speeches. Michael Lee, Keith Langford, Aaron Miles, and especially Wayne Simien gave eloquent speeches that made many in the Fieldhouse well up with tears.

Much like the 2003 National Championship, I didn't get to go to San Antonio for the 2008 Final Four, but I was there in spirit and didn't miss a second of it on TV. And, Dad stayed home for this one so I was able to share in my excitement with Dad, my brothers, and sister. I really loved the game against North Carolina because I wanted to beat Roy Williams so badly, but obviously the win over Memphis, with Mario Chalmers' game-tying shot and subsequent domination in overtime, is the greatest moment for me as a KU fan.

I look forward to each and every year of Kansas basketball. More importantly I have August 17, 2014, circled on my calendar as that will be the day I leave home to begin my academic education at the University of Kansas. My KU basketball education will continue.

Jeanne Mitchell

KU Class of Fall 1996, who now lives in Boulder, Colorado
Jayhawks Here, There, Everywhere!

Most of the events in my life have been shaped by Jayhawk lore. The sunburns at Memorial Stadium, changing over the years from full-on (from sitting in the horseshoe) to left side (student section, with sunglass marks on my cheek) to right side (alumni seats).

The pieces of Jayhawk gear, from sweet baby stocking caps to smallish sweatshirts to sorority letters.

The photos chronicling meeting Big Jay (you can see the man through the mesh) to big-bowed freshmen (me and my dorm mates, so stylish in the early 1990s) to most recently me and my own babies.

Born and bred, they say, and that has surely been the case. My two boys are well on their way, too, with Jayhawk board books, rubber duckies, sippy cups, and tiny football jerseys. These come from all over the country, from the alumni I am so lucky to call family.

Nothing, however, has made any of us so proud as seeing my oldest son, Henry, sharing a laugh with Danny Manning. We met him in January 2009, when the Hawks came to Boulder, Colorado, to play the Buffalos. We were driving to the pre-game party and pulled a U-turn right in downtown Boulder when we spotted Danny Manning crossing the street near his hotel. After completely accosting the man and assailing him with stories of how we watched him score so many points back in 1988, I asked sheepishly if he would pose with my son. Manning was so kind, joking with my little guy and making him giggle, just two guys in on some secret joke. The photo was all the rage, flying around the Internet to acquaintances far and near.

Just two months later, my father passed away. He had started repeating things, a sign of his decline. My father had remarked several times how impressed with the photo he was, how proud he was that I was raising his grandson to be a good Jayhawk. I didn't realize until the funeral how much my dad loved that photo. Literally every person who greeted me said, "Oh, I saw the cutest photo of your son with Danny Manning. Your dad sure did love all of you." Later, I found out from a close friend of my dad's that he had sent everyone he knew the photo not just once, but three times.

Sheryl Miller

I am a student at the University of Kansas, but I had the opportunity to intern at Walt Disney World in Florida in the spring 2009 semester. Although it was a great experience for me, being surrounded by (University of Florida) Gator blue and orange was horrible. I grew desperately homesick for my home on the Hill and the beautiful crimson and blue.

However, within the first few weeks of my internship, I was serving pineapple dole whip to a man in a Jayhawk sweatshirt. Before he left, I said, "Rock Chalk, Jayhawk!" I thought he looked at me funny, but he kind of smiled and went on his way. I was a little disheartened that a fellow fan wouldn't at least acknowledge it, but I figured it was because he was at the Happiest Place on Earth with better things on his mind. Plus, it was unseasonably cold, and who really wants to be held up in line when you could talk to Mickey Mouse instead?

However, within five minutes he was back, this time with his wife and two sons. They stood outside my dole whip stand with their KU shirts and all waved the wheat while chanting the Rock Chalk Chant (even the obviously embarrassed teenage son!) despite the cold and the fact they were on vacation. All my Gator friends working with me just watched in amazement.

It was magical and made my day. For once I didn't feel homesick and realized how truly great KU fans are! It made me even more proud to be a Jayhawk. We really do have the best fan base.

Mario Chalmers celebrating after the Jayhawks won the title in 2008.
Photo courtesy of Jeff Jacobsen/Kansas Athletics

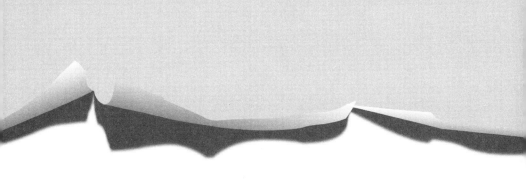

CHAPTER 5

Jayhawk Encounters
of a Unique Kind

Tom Gray

Tom Gray is a longtime Jayhawk Fan, having missed only a handful of home basketball or football games in the past 30 years. He and his "Big 8 Weekend" friends take several "away-game" road trips each year. He has served as president of the Kansas City Chapter of the KU Alumni Association.

Dan DeVine was a good sport.

Photo courtesy of Tom Gray

We have a core group of about five guys who started getting together for the Big 8 basketball tournament weekend. Everyone knows we're going to be having the weekend, so the numbers change every year, but we have five guys who have been doing it for awhile. Of course, it's evolved into Big 12 weekend, and most of the guys are married now. We leave the wives behind and go.

For years, guys would stay in my house, including the year I was going to be in Hawaii with my company. As long as I left the keys behind, they were fine. Eventually, we took it elsewhere after I got married. Our main headquarters now is the Intercontinental Hotel on the Plaza in Kansas City. We usually try to get the concierge level suite with a great view. We have a great time with it.

One year, as it turned out, we were right next to the Missouri athletic department's hospitality room. Their party could not have been any more boring ... and they knew it! One thing they had was food, but they were no fun. So, one by one they started trickling over to our party. A few of us, accompanied by former Kansas City Chiefs player Jonathan Hayes, decided to walk over to K.C. Masterpiece for some barbecue. While we were waiting on our food, we got a call from one of the guys who had stayed behind.

"You won't believe who came to the MU party," he said. "Dan Devine!" We had already ordered dinner that Hayes was going to pay for, but we told the waitress that we'd be right back. We ran out to the car, and went to the hotel as fast as we could because we wanted to see if we could get his autograph. After all, there's no one who's more Missouri than Dan Devine. Of course, he came to our party. He was a great guy. He signed an autograph for us. He was such a great sport that we put a Jayhawk sticker on him and got a picture of him. This was before the Internet, so he probably thought it was no big deal. Well, it ended up in *The Kansas City Star*. He probably never lived it down. But he knew what we were doing. We have a picture of him that shows the sticker. He was posing. That was probably the first and last time he had a Jayhawk on his body.

As a lifelong Jayhawk, I have a lot of great memories, but two top the list. One is when Wilt Chamberlain came back to KU. It was amazing because he told Bob Frederick that he was so touched that, about two-thirds of the way through the game, he told Frederick that he'd sign autographs. He was so moved by the reception he received. He didn't think it would be that great, but it was. We stayed long after the game just to watch. There was a line that was probably five people wide going from him at the free-throw line out the concourse and wrapping around to the door. It was amazing! We were laughing on our way out, thinking there was no way all of those people were going to get something signed. Well, you've probably heard, he was talking to fans and he stayed until every last one of them had an autograph.

The other incredibly poignant moment was when Larry Brown put Archie Marshall in the game for Senior Night.

Archie had been hurt and was on crutches. Out of all my memories, that single moment of Archie coming in after the two tough injuries is the most touching. After the second knee injury, Larry started crying on the air he was so moved by the fact that this happened to Archie. The final game, Senior Night, I looked up and here's Archie, with knee braces, crutches and he's suited up! About a minute or so to go in the game, Larry put Archie in. Of course he could only get to the sideline. Leonard Hamilton, the Oklahoma State coach, motioned for his team to back off so Archie could get the ball. That whole scene was so cool. If you follow his whole story, it's incredible.

John Holt

John Holt comes from a Jayhawk family (his father and four siblings are KU grads). He graduated with a journalism degree in 1981 and a KU law degree in 1984. He's reported and anchored in Topeka, Wichita, and currently in Kansas City at Fox 4-TV.

As someone who comes from a long line of Jayhawks, that Dan Devine story from 1994 that you just read in Tom Gray's feature, is one of my highlights of our annual party. To be at the hotel with all of these KU posters and to find ourselves literally next door to the Missouri hospitality room. Could not have been more delicious. Dan was a great sport. We couldn't believe he was in there. But then again, their party was so bad that even they were coming to our party.

I grew up in Great Bend, Kansas. My dad went to KU, so we would go to Lawrence for games. One of my earliest memories of coming to games was a football game at Memorial Stadium when Nolan Cromwell was playing. We were there the day he got hurt against Oklahoma. We were sitting in the end zone in disbelief. With him out, there was no way KU was going to win. I was devastated because all hope was gone.

Over time, there was no question where I was going to go to school. At that time in Great Bend, though, we were surrounded by K-State fans. That was back in the Jack Hartman/Ted Owens days. Basketball certainly was a rivalry. That was big-time. When I moved to Kansas City to go to work for Fox 4, I had to learn that the main rivalry is KU-MU. You don't get that sense in the middle of Kansas. Even today, out there it's still KU and K-State.

In fact, it was funny, in 1984 a bunch of us went to Manhattan to see KU play basketball at Ahearn. KU hadn't won there since 1980. We were sitting on the window sill upstairs. I remember Carl Henry hitting a jump shot that brought KU from behind and the Hawks ended up winning the game, 63-61. We went downstairs and happened to be there when Coach Larry Brown was leaving the court. He reached out and shook my hand as he headed to the locker room. I thought that was pretty cool. I was flabbergasted. At the time I was working in Topeka. Well, not 30 seconds after getting the hand shake from Larry, an older woman came up to me, wagging her finger in my face. She said — not so nicely — "I watch you on TV and you're a KU fan! I knew I didn't like you!" I was nice about it, but that was the funniest thing. I didn't know what to say. One second I'm high-fiving with my buddies after this win and shaking hands with the coach, and the next an older woman is mad at me because I'm a KU guy. I've often wondered whatever happened to that woman ... and if she ever watched me on the news again.

After working in Topeka, I was in Wichita at the NBC affiliate from 1987-94, right before coming to Kansas City. I came up to Kansas City during Final Four weekend in 1988 to be with our group. We watched the semifinals together, but I had to go back to Wichita on Sunday to go back to work. I was sick about missing the chance to be in Kansas City during the KU-OU game, especially knowing that Monday night, all eyes were going to be on our competitor, CBS, watching the game. Our weather guy, Mike Smith, was an Oklahoma grad. I had to go down to the desk about the time Danny Manning went to the free-throw line with a chance to give KU the definitive lead. This is how I found out what happened in the game while I was on the air. Suddenly out of the corner of my eye, I saw Mike throw down his clipboard in disgust. I knew we had won. About that time, our camera operator, who was a KU guy, peeked out from behind the camera and gave me a thumbs up. Even though I had to work, that was a cool moment that I'll never forget.

What does the "N" on Nebraska's football helmets stand for?

"Nowledge."

I've remained an ardent KU fan. In fact, on football Saturdays, a group of us led by Lindsey Olsen, another huge fan, love to tailgate. For several years, we tailgated in a corner, lot 91. Well, we had to move. Lot 91 is now the site of the new practice facility. We were victims of the football program's success. I guess that's a small price to pay for success.

Chris Reaves

Chris Reaves resided in Lawrence from 1988-97, first as a student and then as a university employee, serving as Special Events Supervisor for campus-wide events. Since 1998, he has worked for Sprint in Kansas City. Chris is also business partners with ex-Kansas City Royals baseball player Greg Pryor in a company called Sportsaholic which specializes in selling Hawkaholic merchandise for die-hard KU fans. Chris resides in Olathe with his "wonderful and supportive wife," Jane.

If there's a great lesson I learned while I was a student at the University of Kansas, it's this: Never go onto the Memorial Stadium field late at night when no one's around. I'll never forget one time several Sigma Phi Epsilon brothers of mine were drinking at our house, as fraternities do on occasion. We had a brilliant idea to take a half-full (or half-empty, depending on how you view life) keg down to Memorial Stadium and sneak into the stadium to play tackle football on the field. To quickly summarize the story, not only was the field like playing on cement, but the Jayhawk logo in the middle was like cement sandpaper. So we were drunk, bleeding, and nobody could score! Trying to kick a field goal was extremely humorous. Of course, that's not the end of the story.

Then the police came (apparently there were sensors on the field that, if tripped, would turn on spotlights on top of the scoreboard). If campus police noticed the spotlights on, they would know someone had sneaked onto the field. We were having fun on the field when all of a sudden we saw several police lights surrounding the stadium. We all scrambled (it seems like there were about seven or eight of us) to get away. I ran to get underneath the stands — and if you have been to Memorial, you know that you are pretty much trapped in the walkthrough under the seats.

Just like in the movies, we see police cars coming down each direction from underneath the stands so while my friends were busy hiding behind pillars and such, I did what I had seen done so many times in the movies ... I jumped in a nearby dumpster. In sober hindsight that was probably the most obvious, dumbest thing to do, but since the police were having a pretty easy time picking off my friends left and right behind pillars like they were on an Easter egg hunt, I never got caught. I waited for what seemed like eternity but was probably just 20 minutes or so. I then climbed out of the dumpster and went sprinting for Potter's Pond, which we had agreed beforehand would be our meeting spot if anything happened.

I remember only one of my fraternity brothers being at Potter's Pond when I got there. We made a long walk back through campus all the way to our fraternity house. When we finally got back, there were several older fraternity brothers who were very upset with us. Not because most of us got arrested for trespassing and public intoxication, but because we left the keg at the 50-yard line!

What makes this story somewhat ironic is that after I graduated from KU, I accepted a job working for the University of Kansas as their Special Events Supervisor, and my office was located under the stands at Memorial Stadium at Gate 25. The best part is they gave me keys to all the gates, which gave me access to the field 24/7. It wasn't until I started working for the university that one of the maintenance guys told me about the sensors at each end zone that triggered the spotlights on the scoreboard.

Of course, once I started working there, a few story-worthy things happened. The basketball office offered university employees first opportunity at purchasing team autographed basketballs for charity for $60. I jumped at the chance and bought approximately 20 balls. I was only making about $19,000 a year back then, but I was straight out of college while most of my friends were still in college making $4 an hour. So, compared to them, I was rich. I decided to buy all these balls and give them as Christmas presents to all my friends and family (for close friend Joe Sorkin, Chanukah present). I actually remember when I handed them out saying that this means I never have to buy them anything again. At that particular time, I might as well have been handing my friends a gold autographed brick.

But back to the story. When the basketball office had finalized my order, Roy Williams' secretary called me to tell me to come to the basketball office to pick up my order. Now you have to understand that at the time, I was probably 23 years old and still star-struck when I would see someone famous. I was walking around the men's basketball office in a daze. I might as well have been in the Smithsonian. I remember just staring at the basketball mural in the main office while the secretary went to get my order. It was pretty funny because I had ordered so many balls that they had to get one of those thick clear plastic tarps and put the balls in the middle and then wrap the clear tarp around them so that they could be carried. So there I was in the men's basketball office, dragging a clear tarp filled with auto-graphed basketballs behind me. I looked like Charles Barkley Claus. As the secretary helped me get through the door, none other than Roy Williams walks up to the door with a VERY puzzled look on his face. After staring at me for a second, he says, and I quote, "Dad-gum it son, you got enough balls?" That was my first encounter with Roy Williams.

I also remember working a basket-ball media day in Lawrence in 1995 for

> **❝ When we finally got back, there were several older fraternity brothers who were very upset with us. Not because most of us got arrested for trespassing and public intoxication, but because we left the keg at the 50-yard line! ❞**

the university. I supplied soft drinks and cookies to the media and hung around for the event. The members of the media were huddled around Jacque Vaughn and Raef LaFrentz. Absolutely NOBODY was talking to this guy named Paul Pierce. I ended up just sitting there eating cookies, talking to him for half of the event.

None of my family or friends were KU fans when I first started becoming a fan around high school. I didn't have any ties to the university. I just remember being drawn to the Jayhawks. I remember watching Ron Kellogg and KU play on Saturdays. Funny that I really don't think of Danny Manning, but instead I always think of Kellogg. He could flat-out shoot. Man, what kind of scoring that guy would have put up if there was a three-point line back then. I became intrigued by KU basketball by watching them play every weekend. I also distinctly remember watching the 1988 National Championship game in Joe Sorkin's parents' basement. (However, I am embarrassed to say that I also remember flipping channels between the game and *Saturday Night Fever*, which was on HBO that night. I have NO flipping clue why. I also remember playing a lot of pool that night and learning to juggle with pool balls. I know, weird memories.) At the time, I had no intentions of going to college, let alone KU. My parents wanted me to enlist in the military. It wasn't until a few weeks before classes started in 1988 that I received a scholarship to go to KU.

I do have many fond memories of attending great history-making games at Allen Fieldhouse over a nine-year span from 1988-97. Ironically, I think the only game I missed during that span was the 150-95 victory over Kentucky. But I was there for the Jacque Vaughn game-winner over Indiana; the huge comeback over UCLA when Ostertag dribbled behind his back down court; Senior Day when Oklahoma State's Bryant Reeves was held to zero points in a KU win; Anthony Peeler's 43-point effort in a loss. Lots of great memories in the Fieldhouse, Memorial Stadium, and even the baseball stadium when I ran the concessions for a year.

Danny, Danny, And, Well, More Danny (And Some Other Legends)

Pete Logan

Lawrence

During my freshman year at KU, 1986-87, I became used to seeing Danny Manning on campus a lot. He had a speech class right before mine at Wescoe and we often saw him at

Pete Logan once "played" with Danny Manning.
Photo courtesy of Pete Logan

Robinson Gymnasium when we went over there to work out or play pickup basketball.

One night, my friends — Pat Valicenti, Dan Yachnin, and Mike Haight — and I went over to Robinson to play some ball. As soon as we walked in, we noticed Danny and Ed Manning (and a few other players and grad assistants) shooting around. They were just two courts down from us. After a couple of quick pickup games on our part, we noticed the Mannings were getting ready to leave. I can't recall whose idea it was but, on a whim, we attempted to sweet talk the Mannings into playing on our team for a game. Danny eventually agreed. We were stoked!

Probably on the advice of his dad and his coaches (well-heeded, I should say) Danny's participation on our team consisted of him standing at center court and distributing passes. He never really moved from that spot and, to this day, I'm glad he didn't. (Imagine the disgrace I would have been to the Jayhawk Nation if I would have conned him into playing and he suffered a devastating injury!) At one point, the future 1988 National Champion did send me a behind-the-back pass. Not everyone can say they got one of those.

Late in the game, we gave the ball to Danny at halfcourt. This time, instead of just giving it up to one of us, he turned with the ball and faced the basket. He took one — maybe two — steps and launched a jumper that went through the basket with a swish upon completing its rainbow-like arc. With that, Danny was off and we were left to find a new fifth. We decided soon after that that we weren't going to top Manning's appearance, so we called it a night and headed back to Oliver Hall.

Mike Hsu

Class of 1993 (now living in Lincoln, Nebraska)

Speaking of Danny Manning, I guess you could say I had a brush with greatness. It was my freshman year at KU in the fall of 1989, and I walked into a convenience store on 23rd St. I went to the fountain to get a Coke when I heard someone say "hello." I turned around, and wouldn't you know it, it was Danny Manning! He must have been back in Lawrence during the NBA off-season. In realizing the one before whom I stood, I responded back with a shaky voice, "Um, hi." But it looked like Danny had been taking some time to talk to the convenience store clerk and that he went out of his way to say hello to little ol' me! I think the reason I didn't see the 6'11" superstar when I first walked into the store was because he had been leaning over the counter, chatting with the clerk. I had always heard that Danny was quiet and reserved and the stories are legendary of Coach (Larry) Brown finding ways to get Danny to be more assertive and vocal. Yet on that day, Danny Manning's friendliness and initiative in going out of his way simply to say "hello" to a freshman kid (and talk to a convenience store manager) is a brief moment in time I will always remember and cherish. Indeed, today as a 38-year-old man, I still cherish the memory as I recount it now.

Logan Bond

Fort Myers, Florida

Like most kids in Kansas around 1988, I was a big Jayhawk fan and an even bigger Danny Manning fan. Well, I had the luck of running into him a few months after they had won the National Championship. My mom had taken me and my brother to an arcade in Overland Park for some video games. We walked in and there was Danny Manning in his USA Olympic jacket playing at one of the games. I couldn't tell at my height, but it seemed as if he was taller than the arcade machines. We waited for him to finish his game and went up and asked for his autograph. He was gracious and signed a yellow sticky note for me and my brother. I still have that sticky note to this day. Many years went by and I grew up to be a decent basketball player myself. I played at Drury University, but still came home in the summers to play in the Kansas City summer league. It was there that I got to play against my idol, Danny Manning. It was after several of his knee surgeries and he may have lost a step by that time, but it was still one of my best basketball memories.

Kirsten Jamison Squitieri

Class of 1992

In the summer of 1991, I was vacationing in Manhattan Beach, California. My friend and I stepped into a bike rental shop off the beach to rent bikes for a ride along the boardwalk.

I had to hand over my driver's license to complete the rental agreement. When I gave the store clerk my Kansas license, he looked at me with surprise and said, "No way! You live in Lawrence, Kansas?"

When I said, "Yes, I am from Kansas." He told me his friend who was in the back of the store used to live in Lawrence. At that, he called into the back room, "Hey,

Danny, come out here, there are some girls here from Lawrence!"

So who pops out from the back room but Danny Manning.

He was really nice and asked us about biking in Lawrence and told us how much he loved biking around Clinton Lake.

He had his baby daughter with him and was putting her on the back of his bike to go for a ride. The three of us biked along the boardwalk together for about 20 minutes and he gave us advice on where else to bike at the beach.

Considering that was just three years after watching "Danny and the Miracles" win the National Championship during my senior year of high school, seeing him that day in California is a great memory!

Bill Lindsay

Class of 1984

The year was 1983 and I was a member of the Kansas University spirit squad. Larry Brown had been hired to turn around a basketball team that had been struggling for several years. Iowa State was the next up on the schedule and the athletic department didn't have a van to get us to Ames for the game. The news got back to Coach Brown that the cheerleaders needed a ride. Apparently it was pretty important to the coach that we make the trip, so he put us on the bus with the players. Riding on the team bus was incredible, and as a KU student I was in heaven. But the story gets even better after we get to Ames.

Anyone who has been to Hilton Coliseum can tell you how loud and crazy the fans can be and how close they are to the floor. During the first half, after KU made a basket, some legs got tangled and one of the Kansas players ended up on the floor. The Iowa State fans were still cheering when just seconds later one of the Cyclone players went face first into the hardwood. None of the refs saw what happened and no fouls were called on either play but the Iowa State fans went crazy and didn't let up until halftime.

In the second half, the Jayhawks kept the score close and if the Iowa State fans were worried they sure didn't show it. They knew the Kansas basketball team had not won a Big 8 road game in over two years. As the clock ticked down, the score stayed close and we continued to cheer on the team, but it was so loud I'm not sure anyone could hear us. With just seconds to go, the final shot went in and Kansas won at the buzzer. The Jayhawk players went crazy, the cheerleaders were jumping up and down, and the Iowa State fans were not happy. It quickly went from boos and jeers to cups and trash being thrown from the stands onto the playing floor.

Coach Brown and the assistant coaches quickly started shuffling the team off the court and then he waved his arm at me to grab the rest of the Spirit Squad and follow the team away from the angry crowd and into the locker room. We screamed and celebrated and then jumped onto the bus for the trip back to Allen Fieldhouse. As a photojournalist at KCTV in Kansas City for the last 25 years, I've been in many locker rooms but I'll never forget that night in Ames, Iowa.

Jennie Bennett

Class of 1977 and KU Alumni Chapter Leader in Tucson, Arizona

I had an encounter, but it wasn't exactly with a Jayhawk. It was after Arizona won the NCAA title in 1997. I had moved to Tucson from Leawood, Kansas, and was very sad that we had not won. But, at a fundraiser, I saw Arizona Coach Lute Olsen and his wife. I went up to them and offered my congratulations on their victory. Coach Olsen asked when I had graduated from the U of A. That's when I confessed that I was a Jayhawk. His wife said, "Wow! What a good sport, let's get a photo," as Lute looked at me in shock!

Dan Barker

My uncle was actually one of the Big Jay mascots for KU. This was when the mascot weighed about 85 pounds. One of my favorite memories — and it was brought up right before my grandmother died — is that my uncle is a very big guy. After he made the mascot squad, he didn't have any mascot boots that would fit him. But, he had really expensive, white cowboy boots. My grandmother kept telling him to take care of the boots. He took care of them, alright. He decided to wear them with his costume. He spray-painted them yellow. The boots were on display at the Booth Hall. As a side note, even though I knew my uncle was in that costume, whenever I saw him in it, it scared the hell out of me.

> ❝ Even though I knew my uncle was in that (Big Jay) costume, whenever I saw him in it, it scared the hell out of me. ❞

Jamie Bilton

Kansas City

I will never forget the electricity surrounding the 1988 Jayhawks' run to the national title. I was in eighth grade that Spring, and completely in awe of Danny and the

Miracles. Looking back now, I can appreciate how this experience—for a 13-year-old Kansas City boy witnessing his favorite local team win the National Championship in his hometown, on the same floor where he'd watched so many other games—was almost too good to be true.

My dad surprised me by picking me up from school on the Friday before the national semifinals and driving me to Kemper Arena (my favorite place in the world) to watch the Final Four teams practice. We sat with several of my buddies, whose dads had conspired to provide the same surprise for their sons. I watched wide-eyed as the Arizona, Duke, Oklahoma, and Kansas teams took turns practicing for about one hour each. The atmosphere was festive and, despite my young age, I had a very real sense that I was experiencing something very special.

After the practice sessions, my dad drove me, my mom, and my brother to the various team hotels — just to see who we could see! We hit one hotel at Crown Center and two more near the Plaza. I'll never forget strolling through the KU hotel lobby that night — what an impression! Several of the players were mingling with fans. I walked right up to my favorite player, point guard Kevin Pritchard, and stuck my right hand out to shake his. "Good luck tomorrow!" I panted eagerly. Pritchard returned my gaze and proceeded to thank me in a very genuine, sincere manner. He could not have been nicer! We saw several other players but I never made it close enough to meet any more. But I was okay with that ... I had met my hero.

Needless to say, watching the Jayhawks defeat Duke and Oklahoma was an immense thrill. I was old enough to realize and understand that they were an underdog in both games. The championship win on Monday night was an amazing cap to an unforgettable weekend.

CHAPTER 6
Sweet Home,
Allen Fieldhouse

Bud Stallworth

Bud Stallworth starred for the Jayhawks from 1970-72, when he became one of the few basketball players in school history to earn All-America honors as a player and as a student. Stallworth went on to a five-year career in the NBA. He moved back to Lawrence in 1987 and recently retired from KU's Design and Construction Management department. Stallworth remains passionate about the Jayhawks and the teams he played on. He'll put his 1971 Final Four team that went 27-3 and lost in the semifinals up against any other Jayhawk team in history. He's still best remembered for his 50-point performance against Missouri in his final game at Allen Fieldhouse, on February 26, 1972.

Bud Stallworth
Photo courtesy of Kansas Athletics Archives

As I was walking to the Fieldhouse for my final game — against Missouri, no less — it was beautiful outside. We were having a disappointing season, but I wasn't going to let Missouri spoil it. Plus, my mom was in Lawrence from Alabama to see me for the first time play in Allen Fieldhouse.

No matter what Missouri did that day, they weren't going to beat us. Now, I had a little extra motivation, too. On the morning of the game, Missouri Coach Norm Stewart had a quote in the paper about how, even though I was having a great individual season, he felt that his player, John Brown, should be Player of the Year in the conference because he was having a better team year than I was having. Norm and

I had a little running narrative during my entire four years. So, it all came down to whether I had enough to get us off and running that day. I guess I did because I scored 50 points. That was one of those days where a lot of things came into play.

I was just so relaxed. Even on my way to the Fieldhouse before the game, I tossed the Frisbee around with some students. Then I got an idea. I took a Frisbee to the locker room. I told the guys that if they signed it, I'd throw it in the stands when I was introduced. Sure enough, I threw that Frisbee in the stands and someone caught it. The last game was important to me. By that time, I had become used to the fans and the hoopla that surrounded the KU program.

Before coming to the University of Kansas as a student in the fall of 1968, I didn't have a clue about the tradition of Jayhawk sports. I didn't know about the fans. The only person I'd heard about from Kansas was Wilt Chamberlain. My oldest sister had come to the Midwestern Music and Arts Camp and then came to KU as a student, but she was in the Fine Arts School, majoring in math and music, so it was not exactly a good reference for the sports at KU. Plus, I'm from Alabama, where we didn't exactly follow the Jayhawks or basketball. Down there, of course, football is king. So, I knew about Wilt and Kansas, had a little knowledge about James Naismith as the inventor of the game, but the real in-depth knowledge about the history of the game and the great players that had come before, I didn't follow it that closely.

It was during the Midwestern Music and Arts Camp that I got noticed to play at KU. My camp counselor called me in one day and asked me if I knew who Ted Owens was. I thought I was in trouble. I said, "Whatever he says I did, I didn't do it." He told me that Ted was the basketball coach. I knew that some of the guys we were playing with had played on the KU team, but it wasn't a big deal because I didn't know much about the team. Come to find out, Jo Jo White was one of the guys playing in the group, and he told Ted about this high school kid who was tearing it up against some of the college players. Ted called me in. The first thing I did was ask him to not tell my dad I was playing basketball during band camp. We talked for a little bit, and Sam Miranda, Ted's assistant coach, came and watched me play during my senior year. They offered me a scholarship at that time and I took it immediately.

When I got here in 1968 for my freshman year, I got to spend time with varsity because they were in summer school, like Jo Jo, Dave Nash, and those guys that were on the 1966 team that went to the Final Four. I knew about the game they had lost to Texas Western and then how Texas Western beat Kentucky for the National Championship, but I didn't know about how big of a game it was and how upset the Jayhawks were about losing that game.

Going into my freshman year, I had to play on the freshman team, so I watched the varsity, watched the fans, and read about the history of Kansas basketball. I was close to Jo Jo and how great of a player he was recognized as being. Then I started to study more and realize how big of a deal it was not only to play there — because when I had been recruited, the coaches told me about the history, the opportunity to play for a National Championship, and the players that came before me. But as a youngster and coming into that environment, you didn't know the magnitude of it until you stepped into it. Then it's like, "OK, this is a big deal." Even though I heard about Dr. Naismith, I didn't know he was the first coach, I didn't know he had lived in Lawrence and then coached here, and the next coach was Phog Allen. They had a couple coaches before Coach Owens was the coach. You thought about the tradition and how many people had come through the program and all of the great players besides Wilt. They had All-Americas and championships going back to the 1920s. So it became more of an awakening for me to get a chance to really understand what the coaches were talking about: having an opportunity to play basketball at Kansas University is a big deal. And you have to understand it is one of the great universities, especially for basketball, in the country.

My first varsity game in Allen Fieldhouse, in front of that amazing crowd, was on December 1, 1969. That was my sophomore year. As a freshman team, when we came out, there might have been a few fans. We were the warm up. I saw the guys run out. Back then, what really got me was the chance to run through that big paper hoop that the team burst through. When you do that, the fight song starts up and the pregame hype goes nuts. That's what I wanted a chance to do. How did they feel coming out of that tunnel, bursting onto the court, with the Jayhawk pep band playing our fight song and the crowd going wild? My anticipation of being able to do that was one of the most important things on my mind going into my sophomore year. I could envision it because I imagined it. That was the ultimate — running onto the court through that paper hula hoop. It had to be one of the most fascinating things I'd seen.

You have to understand, when I came from Alabama, we played in a little gym, and I didn't even play in a gym until my sophomore year. So, playing in the gym that held maybe 150 people, and then seeing (back then) close to 17,000, filling the seats in Allen Fieldhouse, that was pretty impressive for a guy from a small town. Then, you could come through that tunnel and everyone was waiting for you to burst through that paper, that was the cat's meow for me.

Finally doing that was everything and then some. I started as a sophomore so I got a chance to burst through there not only during the first home game, but then, the real big deal was hearing them call my name for the starting line-up. When I had a chance to do all of

> **" That was the ultimate — running onto the court through that paper hula hoop. "**

that, I thought I'd died and gone to heaven. All of the things that I'd dreamed about — playing basketball at a major university, starting for that major university, and to top it off, playing at one that had a chance to win the National Championship, that was it. All of those things from when I was in my backyard and playing against Oscar Robertson or Jerry West, or even Wilt, who had to guard me sometimes ... I've had all of that in my mind. Then, having it come around; this is what it's all about. I just had to see what I could do with it.

I absolutely remember that first varsity game. I was 19 and I can still feel that adrenaline of coming through the tunnel. We played Marshall University. At that time, I scored more points than any sophomore in his debut game. I scored 27. I got off to a pretty good start and developed a good rapport with the fans.

The KU fans were — and still are — the best. They would bring the banners that read: "When you say Bud, you've said it all." And the band would play the beer commercial jingle. Our junior year, when we won the Big 8 at home, was huge. We used to have a preseason Christmas tournament and we won it the first two years I played. We didn't allow many teams to come into the Fieldhouse and beat us. That was impressive because the fans were so good. I can never remember fans booing a KU player at home to this day. That's amazing. You can go to some places and hear fans boo a few of their home players. At KU, you never hear the fans boo the players while they're playing at the University of Kansas, which says a lot for the fans and the program.

Today, fans have some help when intimidating opposing players. When you have a loud video going on before the game that could shake steel and foundation, you're going to generate more excitement. We had a pep band and the fans beating on their seats. That was it. Enthusiasm was just as good, and we played in front of sell-out crowds. The fans have more things to generate fan interaction but if you measured the decibel levels, the Fieldhouse was loud back then.

The crowd was loud and intimidating to teams coming in. I remember in my junior year, we opened at home against Long Beach, which was the preseason No. 1 team. They came in the Fieldhouse during our practice. They were walking around the court, looking around, and they were in awe. I guess they imagined that we played in a barn or something. At that time, it was one of the lowest scores we'd held a team at home in a half. They were stunned. They thought they were coming in to play a bunch of country guys and blow us out. We ended up beating them, 69-52.

All of that said, teams are more intimidated of playing at Allen Fieldhouse today. When I sit in the stands for a game, the first thing I do is watch the visitor's bench. And it's something; if I have someone with me who hasn't been to the Fieldhouse, I tell them to watch. Usually, coaches try to get their guys not to look around. Once they pay attention to the tradition, and the volume of the fans, and the highlights that play on the video board, that's going to take away from the kids. He'll start to think, "Oh, my goodness! Is this what we have to deal with?" (They don't realize that most of the guys playing today aren't even in that video.) The drama, the mystique and the fans almost cracking windows, you have a home-court advantage. Maybe some of the Big 12 teams are more immune to it, but the non-conference opponents coming in there, if you look at that bench, those guys are trying to sneak looks at the video. Their coaches definitely don't want them watching it.

One of the greatest days in the Fieldhouse was when Wilt Chamberlain returned. A lot of people didn't understand why Wilt was the way he was. He was a guy, though, who thought he should win every game and every championship. One of the saddest things about it all is that he didn't get back to Lawrence earlier and more often. It definitely brought out his tears, and they were genuine because he realized he missed all of that. He missed that people loved him, respected him, and admired the things he accomplished. He was always going to be a Jayhawk, no matter what. Nothing was going to change that. Once he came back and saw that and felt that, he wanted to spend time signing autographs, which he did for hours after the game. Usually a guy of that magnitude might sign for 30-45 minutes. But Wilt sat down and signed every last autograph. I don't know how long he was there, but it was much longer than 45 minutes.

Even though he was the one Jayhawk I knew of before I came to Kansas, the first time I met Wilt wasn't until my first professional game. We played the Lakers, and Wilt was L.A.'s starting center. During the pregame warm ups, I went over and introduced myself to him. He acknowledged that he knew who I was, although I don't know if he was telling the truth. Jokingly, right before the tip, Wilt told the referee, "Don't call any fouls, don't call three seconds, and don't call any goaltending." I was standing there thinking, "Are you kidding me? Is that why you never foul out of a game?" Years after that, I owned a restaurant in California, and I had a chance to visit with Wilt a few times. One time, KU was out there playing either UCLA or USC, and I saw him at that game. So, I ran across him a few times before he returned to Lawrence.

I think Wilt felt like he guaranteed something and he wasn't able to fulfill it. I don't think he understood that KU fans don't blame one player for a win or a loss, even when it's the National Championship. They accept it and they move on because they truly understand the nature of the game. They know that the guys who wear the KU uniforms are not only some of the best players in college basketball, but also some of the ones who give effort all of the time. I think the fan base is why you can recruit guys well at the University of Kansas. Guys know that they're going to get an audience that will support them, 100 percent, no matter what.

These days, I'm one of those passionate fans. I moved back to Lawrence in 1987, just in time for the National Championship (in 1988). So, I was in Kemper Arena for the Final Four. I left that building without a voice because I was cheering so loudly. I told Danny Manning recently that one of the most impressive halves of basketball for a spectator to watch was the first half of the KU-OU title game. Other memories stand out as a fan. The time we came back against UCLA, when they had a huge lead, and beat them. The time Jacque Vaughn hit the last-second shot that beat Indiana. And, of course, the game when Nick Collison got off against Texas with 24 points and 23 rebounds. And, some opponents have come in to the Fieldhouse and had some big games. In the last 10-15 years, we've had some tremendous individual games for both KU players and some opponents. I'm a fan in that way. But I'm always hoping KU wins the game. Hey, you can play great, just don't beat us.

Then there's the 2008 championship team. I get to as many home and away games as I can. But to be in San Antonio, and seeing those guys not give up when they could've easily rolled over

> **"Hey, I got that Frisbee in my divorce!"**

and decided they just didn't have it that game, that Memphis was just better. They kept fighting. I was sitting around a bunch of former KU players. When Mario hit that shot, I told them that Memphis was beat. They couldn't come back and play after that. Sitting there, watching that celebration, that topped it off for awhile. (Although now I want another two or three championships.)

It's great to be a Jayhawk!

By the way, going back to my career, the fans, and that 50-point game against Missouri — which we won, 93-80 — and the signed Frisbee that I threw into the stands during the introductions. Years later, I was at a football game in Lawrence, and a lady came up to me saying, "Hey, I got that Frisbee in my divorce!"

We had a great time with the fans. As an old guy who's been around Lawrence longer than I anticipated, having that appreciation for what our teams accomplished and now to enjoy it as a fan, is what living is all about. The fans are one reason that it's so great to continue living in Lawrence.

Ryan Bauer

Ryan Bauer, 2004 graduate, has been a KU fan his entire life. He says, "The best part about being a Jayhawk is you'll always be better than Mizzou." Incidentally, Ryan is a grandson of former major-league baseball great and World War II hero, Hank Bauer. (And, whether by coincidence or his natural superstitions, Ryan's original story for this book was 2,008 words long.)

Monday, April 7, 2008. This day presented the opportunity to wash away so many moments of being so close. So many moments of questioning, "How did we lose that one?" I knew when I woke up that morning that I would be repeating the phrase "tonight is the night" throughout the day to my best friends, my mom, strangers, and even the guy at the fast food taco place that evening.

I was raised on KU hoops. From the womb, this was all I knew. So the anticipation and excitement were immense to say the least.

Being superstitious, I went to painful lengths to ensure that I didn't repeat anything from the 1991 or 2003 seasons. No shooting hoops in the driveway like I did in 1991. No e-mail to my dad (my favorite KU fan of all time) like I did in 2003, detailing how this was the year and how we were due for a championship. And no reading the papers like I did in years prior.

Leading up to the 2008 tournament, I created a new superstitious routine. Before the first round, I set the wake-up track on my CD alarm clock to No. 6, the number of wins it would take to cut down the nets in San Antonio. I changed it to track 5 before the UNLV game, and so on and so forth. And since I had no reason to wake up early on Sunday, the day before the national championship, I only woke up to track 1.

Since our first tournament game in Omaha against Portland State, I made sure to wear the same socks on game days against UNLV, Villanova, Davidson, and the trashing of North Carolina. It was a good thing that this was the final game because even before the Sweet 16, my socks had a huge and quite noticeable hole in the right heel.

For each game and for the grand finale, I wore the same undershirt that now had sweat rings in the neck from the stressful rigors of the Big Dance. And, of course, during the work day, I wore the same tie. It is adorned with Jayhawks and serves as a public proclamation of my allegiances, where my heart and soul were overly invested, a symbol of who I am.

> A Mizzou fan walks into a store and says, "I'd like some black pants, a gold shirt, and a striped hat."
> The store clerk says, "Are you a Mizzou fan?"
> The fan says, "Yes! Could you tell by the color combination?"
> "No," the clerk says. "This is a hardware store."

The same suit, the same shoes ... well, you get it.

Being too young to appreciate the 1988 title and being upset in 1991 and left emotionally damaged in 2003, I had thought every day about what would happen when the final horn sounded and there my alma mater was, the last team standing, the greatest, the undeniable best. I had turned down a car for my 16th birthday — instead, I got a ticket to the Sweet 16 game against Arizona in 1997. That was the best team I have ever seen. How they could NOT win the title? Well, I'm still not sure, but I watched them get eliminated. Thankfully, I have a lot of blind faith in my Jayhawks and have been able to convince myself that every year is the year. And 2008 was no different. Except that it was.

I really thought I would be discussing this ultimate accomplishment five years earlier when my favorite player of all time, Kirk Hinrich, was leading the Jayhawks to a route of Marquette in the national semifinal. As you know, March Madness went a little late that year and turned into April chaos with the loss to Syracuse and then the whole Roy Williams fiasco. It kind of made me think it might be a little while before we got back. That's when I was thinking pessimistically, but without that loss and all the others, this wouldn't be so sweet.

Everybody has their favorites on every team and their all-time favorites. For this team, it was Russell Robinson. To me, he embodied what Bill Self wanted Kansas basketball to be. Not flashy but extremely tough. Determined and confident, not cocky. He was the glue that would keep this high-tech machine of a team together. At the time it was hard to see exactly how talented the 2008 team was because there weren't the surefire All-Americas like Hinrich and Nick Collison from 2003 and Drew Gooden the year before that. As we found out, though, this team was spilling over with talent and they all gave of themselves to do one thing — WIN. That made the whole thing special.

What does the "O" on Oklahoma's football helmets stand for?

"Onor."

The culmination of this season of Kansas basketball was so great for the fans because we were treated to a magical season of football by Mark Mangino's squad. As they marched to an 11-0 start, it was harder to get excited about basketball games against UMKC, Yale, and DePaul, partly because everyone expected KU to win and partly because we had something to still emotionally invest in that fall. So as the final night arrived there was a little something extra going on, the possibility to complete the greatest year of KU athletics ever.

I had it all figured out. I would drop to my knees and with two closed fists bang the floor and scream, "Finally!" That's what I would do when the final buzzer sounded and minutes before "One Shining Moment" was actually worth watching for once.

After that, the one thing I wanted to do was call my dad, the guy who said forget it to "Itsy Bitsy Spider," because as his only son, his first child, he wanted to teach the Rock Chalk chant. That's who I wanted to talk to; we've been through it all together and we needed to celebrate together.

However, this night went exactly as planned ... and not really.

I had planned on watching the game by myself, but my sister, who was a senior at KU, sent me a text message. It roughly read, "You'll regret this if you aren't in Lawrence."

So I left the impromptu happy hour in Overland Park and put on my lucky shirt, my lucky jeans, my lucky KU shoes, and the same socks as I had for the previous five tournament games.

I got in my car and headed to Lawrence. I don't remember a single second of that drive except that I said this is the last drive I will make to Lawrence without being a national champion.

I think I did what every longtime KU fan would do. I soaked up the moment, making sure I drove down Massachusetts Street before it was mobbed by 50,000 jovial KU fans elated with the brand new National Championship.

Then I headed to Allen Fieldhouse after I parked in the same parking lot I had parked in as an undergrad and for every KU football and basketball game for as long as I can remember.

With the freedom to choose my seat, I sat right under-neath the 1988 National Championship banner, the same banner I had gazed at during every national anthem since I can remember. This was good karma. Plus, it had the added bonus of not having to strain my neck to watch the video board. I said I'm a diehard — I didn't say I wasn't a wuss!

The first time I ever stepped foot in Allen Fieldhouse for "Late Night with Roy Williams" on Halloween in 1992, I never thought that I would be sitting there again for the hundredth time or so watching the national championship game on a video board, and maybe that's because there wasn't a video board in 1992. The changes to Allen were many since 1992, but the feelings that one gets when they are in this museum of basketball greatness never do.

At the first TV timeout with KU trailing, I remember telling my sister that if we win the next four minutes and just play every four minutes at a time, we'd be in great shape. This was mostly to calm myself down and not dive off the deep end.

Fast forward to 2:12 left in the game. I tell my sister we should trade places; instead of me on her left, she is now standing to my left.

"He's going to miss this free throw," I said, and Chris Douglas Roberts obliged. Memphis missing free throws was great, but I was in quite a bit of pain during it all, physical pain. I was standing with my right leg on the ground and my left leg up and pressed against the wall behind me, which after awhile gets a little uncomfortable. But I did this and Memphis missed a free throw, so I just stayed that way.

An 18-foot jumper by Darrell "Shady" Arthur cut it to seven, you remember.

A high-five without making eye contact.

A steal, a three, it's GOOD!

KU is down four and has a chance.

Fast-forward to Derrick Rose making the second of two charities to make it a three-point game.

A little perspective — my sister hasn't cried in four years, a personal vow of strength to herself, so here we are 10.2 seconds left and the inbounds to Sherron Collins.

The flip to Mario Chalmers, a shot — MONEY, a shot so pure it didn't even think about touching the rim.

Being completely consumed in the game I had to make sure Memphis missed their desperation shot and they did.

OVERTIME!

At that moment, I threw my sister in the air, tears streaming down her face, overwhelmed in the moment that would change the lives of KU fans, everywhere, forever.

I lost myself for a minute in what had just happened: "Mario's Miracle!" Finally, on the right side of things, for once.

I knew at that moment I was going to be celebrating a National Championship, very soon. And before overtime could tip, I made eye contact with my future wife and winked and nodded my head, because I can only marry someone who knows what that means: "It's on, this game is ours, close out, win this thing, five more minutes."

And then it happened, hoop after hoop after hoop. KU scored however it wanted and drained the shot clock down to 1 second before Darnell Jackson made a lay-in to give KU a six-point lead.

Here it was, this close to what I have wanted for so long.

On the doorstep of "No one can say anything, because we're the best." Just around the block from "Raise another banner."

Here we were, the Jayhawk Nation, ready for what we had wanted, deserved, felt entitled to, for so long.

When Arthur snagged his 10th rebound, eight fewer than his assistant coach, Danny Manning, had grabbed when Darrell was not even one year old, and threw the ball to Sherron Collins, the question of who would dribble out our National Championship was answered.

It was the guy Bill Self said was the "missing piece to a National Championship," Sherron Collins.

And there in Allen Fieldhouse, hundreds of miles away from San Antonio, students storming the court, the tingling feeling of "I'm not even sure what just happened."

Jayhawk fans everywhere, who had lived through so many disappointments in 20 years, were finally granted our wish — a National Championship.

Less than 48 hours short of my 27th birthday, my inadequacies were removed. My blind faith rewarded.

I went from being 5'6" to feeling tall, feeling strong when I was physically weak, excellent when all signs pointed to average.

This was what I had wanted for so long.

And when it has been forever you don't know what to do. You're happy it happened, but what was premeditated is now lost.

You lose yourself in the moment. You enjoy it like Christmas is happening twice at the same time. This year, though, there was no coal in our stockings. No ugly sweater from the crazy aunt.

All you got was everything you ever wanted. In the words of (CBS broadcaster) Jim Nantz, a "Rock Chalk Championship."

Craig Brown

KU Class of 1993

"BEWARE OF THE PHOG"

One of my first games at the Fieldhouse was the beatdown of Kentucky in 1989, when KU scored 150 points. A few years later, KU played an overmatched Siena squad and hung something like 140 points on them. After the game, I commented to then-Sports Information Director Dean Buchan that I thought the Hawks had a shot at breaking the Kentucky record. Dean gave me a knowing smile and said, "That record won't be broken in a game against Siena." Nice! The message was pretty clear.

I also recall the Missouri game when Anthony Peeler went for 43 points, which is the most amazing performance I've ever seen at the Fieldhouse by an opposing player. (It hurts to say that.)

As sports director at KJHK while I was in school, I was careful never to abuse the station's media credentials. But after I graduated in December of 1993, I couldn't resist. Although the station was off the air for Christmas, and we didn't have a seat on the press row, I "borrowed" the station's credentials to get into the Indiana game. What an awesome game! That was the game when freshman Jacque Vaughn hit a three-pointer at the buzzer, giving KU an 86-83 win. I don't think the Fieldhouse was ever as loud as it was that evening. A perfect way for me to close out my student career at KU.

Laura Carpenter

KU Class of 1995, Architectural Engineering

Early in the 1993-94 basketball season, my twin sister was visiting from another Big 8 Conference school — Colorado — and I thought it would be fun to take her to a game at Allen Fieldhouse. I found an extra ticket for Lisa, and had her go in early with one of my friends to save some seats. I couldn't go early, so I told her I would meet them later.

Lisa was amazed at the energy, excitement, and noise that the KU fans generated in the Fieldhouse. She noticed a guy that was wearing a really cool Allen Fieldhouse T-shirt and was openly staring at him, hoping to purchase a shirt like that for our father, a KU alum. Coincidentally, the shirt guy kept waving to someone near where Lisa and my friend were sitting. Lisa kept looking around to see who the T-shirt man was waving at, but never saw anyone waving back. T-shirt Man starting walking up the stairs in Lisa's direction, and she was excited that she was going to get a closer look at his shirt. Instead of walking by, he turned down her aisle and promptly sat down on her lap! Lisa was more than a little shocked. T-shirt Man immediately said, still on her lap, "I have been waving to you for the past five minutes and you act like you don't even know who I am!" My friend started to laugh, realizing he must think Lisa was me, and was tapping him on his shoulder very patiently while he continued giving Lisa a piece of his mind. As it turns out, he was a study partner of mine from a surveying class that semester. My friend finally got his attention and introduced him to Lisa, my twin. He jumped right off her lap, apologized for his tirade, and made his way back to his seat.

The Carpenter twins at Allen Fieldhouse.
Photo courtesy of Laura Carpenter

I finally made it to the Fieldhouse. When I found Lisa and my friend, they were laughing and told me about the confusion. Needless to say, we all got a big laugh out of it. My sister found out I had some pretty funny and rather "forward" classmates.

The best part of the game that night was watching Jacque Vaughn (a freshman that year) put in the last three-point shot to beat Indiana. The crowd roared! BEWARE OF THE PHOG! My sister had never experienced a better basketball game and found out why KU has such a deep tradition. She said CU basketball was just never the same to her. Poor Buffs.

Ryan Gordon

Class of 2000

Growing up, I was always a huge KU basketball fan. In eighth grade, I had the opportunity to see my first game in Allen Fieldhouse. It was December 9, 1989, the day KU beat Kentucky, 150-95. I knew that day I would be attending the University of Kansas.

My freshman year at KU was the 1994-95 season. I was so excited to see my first game as a student that I showed up very early to the Fieldhouse with my friend and roommate, Ryan Friedman. Very early ... as in hours before. We both had student tickets, but as it turned out they would never get torn because we got there when the workers were showing up. As we were walking around the Fieldhouse, we noticed that with all of the concession vendors, media, and support staff working in there before the game that nobody cared that we were inside looking around. Security did lock the doors to the public eventually, but we were already inside. We walked around for a while longer and realized they would be letting the students in to take seats soon. We saw an opportunity to get REALLY good seats!

So, we found a place and hid out. There was a very large wooden box on its side under the bleachers in one of the high corners of the building. My guess is that it was used as a camera stand and stored there when not used, but that is only a guess. For whatever reason, it was under the bleachers and provided a perfect place to hide. After an hour or so, we heard screaming, excited students running for seats. We quickly escaped our location and ran down to the middle of the seat-getting frenzy. We ran to great seats in the front row of the student section behind the home bench.

We repeated this exercise for the entire season, sometimes showing up several hours before the game to make sure we could go inside the Fieldhouse undetected. It became a mandatory ritual as the Jayhawks continued their home winning streak and eventually went undefeated.

As a side note: One game we sat right behind my childhood hero, George Brett. Covering him with confetti during the pre-game lineup announcements is one of the highlights of my time at KU.

Mic Johnson

Prairie Village, Kansas

I have a few favorite memories of Allen Fieldhouse. One was Adonis Jordan's Senior Night speech. He ended it with, "Peace out. I love everybody."

Another memory I have of Allen Fieldhouse was during my junior year at KU. I got selected for one of the halftime contests where you shoot several shots to get as many points as you can in the allotted time. Unfortunately, you don't get to warm up before you start shooting and that was evident by my "performance." I shot a couple of short ones and a free throw or two, but then I got greedy. I reeeeaaaalllly wanted to sink a three-pointer and hear the Allen Fieldhouse crowd roar. I was launching three after three and never hit one. However, I did miss a three so badly that it slammed the backboard and bounced back near me. I took my right hand and flipped it around my back to set me up for the next three-point shot. Apparently, that "sleight of hand" briefly got the crowd's attention and I heard a somewhat mocking "Wooooooooooooooooo" from the Allen Fieldhouse faithful. It wasn't the roar I was hoping for, but a "Wooooooooooooooooo" is better than nothing.

CHAPTER 7
The Magic of Wilt

"A little over 40 years ago, I lost what I thought was the toughest battle in sports, in losing to the North Carolina Tar Heels by one point in triple-overtime. It was a devastating thing for me because I felt as though I let the University of Kansas down and my teammates down. But when I came back here today, I realize that it was just a loss of a game by how many people have shown me so much appreciation and love and warmth from the University of Kansas. [Pauses for 15 seconds because of the ovation.] I've learned ... I've learned over the years that you must learn to take the bitter with the sweet — and how sweet this is right here. I'm telling you. This is really ... I'm a Jayhawk and I know now why there's so much tradition here, and so many wonderful things have come from here, and I'm now very much a part of it by [having No. 13 retired] and very proud of it. Rock Chalk, Jayhawk!"

— Wilt Chamberlain's speech when his jersey was retired at Allen Fieldhouse on January 17, 1998. Chamberlain passed away on October 12, 1999. Then, in 2003, it was announced that Chamberlain's estate had donated $650,000 to the University of Kansas to endow three scholarships and a Special Olympics program.

*Speech used with permission of the University of Kansas Athletic Department.

Vince Brown

Vince Brown grew up three blocks from his grade school, Cordley Elementary, six or seven blocks from Central Junior High, one block from Lawrence High and just down the hill from the Chancellor's residence on the KU campus. He says it was a great neighborhood and a great way to grow up. "The first time I was on another major university campus it was flat," he added. "It felt odd. There were no clear lines of demarcation. No majesty. As a kid, the Hill was the way campuses were supposed to be. In some ways, I'm still a kid."

Vince Brown

Photo courtesy of Vince Brown

Until I was six years old, my mother and I lived with my grandmother in her house in the 1700 block of Ohio Street. At the time, Grandma, Alberta Frye, was the cook for the medical fraternity on Indiana Street and housemother for the Alpha Phi Alpha fraternity on Mississippi Street, across from Memorial Stadium. One weekend evening, the Kappas, the other black fraternity on campus, were having a party to which Grandma had been invited as a chaperone. Her ride came to the house to pick her up. I was off playing somewhere in the house when my mother called, "Vincent, come meet Mr. Chamberlain!" I didn't really know who "Mr. Chamberlain" was at the time. At age six, other things were even bigger to me than a 7'1" Jayhawk. The only thing I'm sure of is that when he shook my hand, most of my arm disappeared. To this day I don't remember seeing his face. It was a long way up there for a little kid. They tell me after shaking Wilt's hand, I ran off, maybe even hid somewhere. I really wish I'd gotten to tell Mr. Chamberlain this story.

I also had a Big Brother (KU-Y, then, I believe) starting in the sixth grade. (For some reason, administrators thought I was incorrigible.) My Big Brother was Nolen Ellison, captain of the KU basketball team in 1962-63. That made me somewhat of a celebrity at Cordley Elementary School. Funny thing, I don't remember ever seeing Nolen play. I had Nolen's photo on my bedroom wall along with Jim Dumas,

Riney Lochmann, Jerry Gardner, Delvin Lewis, and others. Nolen graduated and handed me off to another volunteer. I was in junior high when I'd use his student ID and wear his hat and coat to get into games free. I remember, too, wearing the giant KUBB — KU Basketball Booster — button to get into games. (KUFF — KU Football Fan — was the fall equivalent.) Those buttons were huge! This second "sibling" and I stayed friends for years. He left KU to teach in Colorado. Funny thing, but he and his family moved to Arizona years later, and they lived about four blocks from me, and our friendship renewed.

I'm 58 years old and can't remember when I wasn't a KU fan. Growing up, my mother, grandmother, and both of my grandmother's sisters were cooks in the Greek system. Most other adult males whose jobs I was aware of worked on the Hill, too (Grandma's brother, John, worked at the Student Union and brother Alfred cooked for the athletic teams). To me the most meaningful of those connections was Ralph Thomas, who worked in the power plant. His step-daughter, Gwen, was my Godmother and my mother's best friend from childhood. Ralph was my father figure. He taught me how to ride my bicycle, fixed my baseball glove, and we used to watch the Friday Night Fights with the Gillette Bluebird announcing the rounds. When I was very young I'd sit in his lap as each three-minute round went by. Too bad boxing isn't like that anymore. I knew when the whistle blew at 5 p.m. that Ralph would be rounding the corner at 17th and Ohio shortly thereafter. Many times I'd be waiting for him and we'd walk that last half block together.

When I was older, during the John Hadl, Curtis McClinton, and Bert Coan era, I could hear the crowd noise in my back yard at 1743 Ohio St. whenever KU made a big play. I'd be playing with my dog or raking/burning leaves as the noise would roll up from the stadium and down into my back yard. That's a Rockwellian scene: a young boy, his dog, and a pile of dried leaves on a Saturday afternoon. Those two memories — the aroma of burning leaves and the cheering crowd — are inseparable. I'd have to say that seeing that stadium so frequently at an early age was the beginning of my addiction to KU athletics.

I wish I could remember my first game at either Memorial Stadium or Allen Fieldhouse. All I can say is that the feeling of watching a game in either venue, but especially in the Fieldhouse, falls under the category of: "If you have to ask, I can't explain it to you." People who think they have experienced fan loyalty and passion have not been in the Fieldhouse for an MU game. There are ghosts in that building. "The Phog" is real. It doesn't matter what anyone says. It doesn't matter how many championships other schools may have. Mt. Oread, after Springfield, Massachusetts, was the first major stop on the road that college basketball has taken. James Naismith came to Lawrence, Kansas! He is still in Lawrence. As time passes, the names of previous NCAA title winners and the year in which they accomplished that goal fades. The name on the Allen Fieldhouse court doesn't fade.

What did the average Missouri player get on his S.A.T.?

Drool.

The T-shirt I saw during the 2008 Final Four said it best: "Kansas, birthplace of North Carolina basketball." Each of the other three teams in that Final Four — North Carolina, UCLA, Memphis — had KU connections. There could be several versions of that shirt. Either way, with Dr. Naismith, the game's inventor, going from Springfield to Lawrence, it's hard for any school to debate the birthplace of college basketball.

Speaking of Memorial Stadium, though, I do remember some of the games I got to "broadcast" from there. My best friend John and I, on occasion, would get into the old press box and pretend to call a game. It was far from being secure. The stadium was open and we'd ride our bicycles up there and create memories. We might not be as good as Max Falkenstien, but we thought we were pretty good.

Seems during the fall, we were either "broadcasting" football games or "playing" games with Gale Sayers as the star. He was the one for KU then. In those days kids could line up before the game and possibly get chosen to sell drinks and snacks during the game. You could make some good money if you worked hard. I didn't care about the money. I was there to see Gale Sayers do his thing, which he did regularly. The downside is that I missed his opening kickoff return against OU. I had sold all my Cokes and was under the stadium stocking up. As I came back into the stadium my junior high science teacher was yelling, "Sayers ran it back!" He saw it. Maybe that's why I never really liked him.

During Sayers' 22-touchdown (NFL) rookie season, he had that six-touchdown game against the San Francisco 49ers. That was a special day for me: December 12, 1965, because it was my 15th birthday. Sayers' six touchdowns weren't quite like Babe Ruth hitting a home run for a sick child, but I can pretend Sayers did that for me. The irony is that the injury that contributed greatly to Sayers' short NFL career also occurred against the 49ers. A hit by Kermit Alexander tore up his knee.

As far as other football seasons, the 1968-69 Orange Bowl campaign is memorable because it was my freshman year and the last time for 30-plus years that KU defeated Nebraska. I had tickets for the 2005 KU-NU game when the

The KU colors have been flying proudly with recent success in both football and basketball.

Photo courtesy of Jeff Jacobsen/Kansas Athletics

Hawks finally came out on the winning end. I made sure I had plenty of time to get to Lawrence from Overland Park, Kansas, got dressed, loaded my car, checked to make sure I had the tickets, got in the car, and turned the key. All I heard was the silence that resulted from my dead battery! I missed the game. I missed the chance to be at the beginning and the end of the losing streak. But I was in my seat when KU dominated Nebraska, 76-39, in 2007! Outstanding.

Of course, there's also basketball. The 1987-88 season stands out for any KU fan for obvious reasons. I was living in Arizona at the time and knew that the Hawks weren't having a great season. Injuries and losses seemed to be piling up so I didn't follow the team as closely as usual. Sad to say, but I didn't realize they were in the NCAA tournament until they had won two games! That's when I started hearing from the Arizona fans. I wouldn't respond to their comments. Not my style. However, after OU beat the Wildcats and KU knocked off Duke in the semifinals, I wore as much KU gear as I could to work the next day. I watched the KU-OU game by myself because I didn't want to listen to non-believers. Once again, most of my KU gear came out the next day.

When it comes to KU basketball players, even though he didn't win a title, Wilt remains No. 1 on my court. I must have seen Nolen play, but as I said, I can't remember any games with him. Jo Jo White could get down the floor faster with the ball than most players could without it. Then there's Pierre Russell. Jerod Haase may have written "Floor Burns," but Russell left flesh on the floor years before. And who could forget Walt Wesley? I was in junior high and would attend games with friends wearing our giant KUBB buttons. (A medieval knight could have used one as a shield!) I can remember sitting at the end of the old raised basketball floor watching Wesley rip rebounds from the air.

A few years ago, I was at a football game sitting high in the east stands. Across the aisle were about 20 members of Alpha Phi Alpha who were in town for a reunion, including Wesley. Right as the game ended and he stood up to leave, I approached him, introduced myself and said simply, "Thanks for the memories." Looking back, it was inadequate, but all I could muster when faced with a childhood idol.

Earlier in that game, I had introduced myself to one fellow sitting across from me and asked if there was anyone in attendance from the 1950s. There was only one. Wilbur Goodseal. That was a treat for me because he was one who Alberta often mentioned when speaking of "her boys." His face lit up when I mentioned her name. It's a moment I won't forget. When it comes to KU and Grandma, there are a lot of moments I'll never forget.

D. Pearce

Short Tales of a Tall Man

When I was a sophomore in high school, our small town of Gardner, Kansas, held our prom at the student union on the KU campus. While hanging out in the lobby, to our surprise, came the basketball star, Wilt "the Stilt" Chamberlain. My boyfriend, who was a senior and a jock, recognized Chamberlain — but then again, he did stand out a little because he was so big. He very graciously gave us his autograph and talked with us for a bit. As I reflect on that, I am surprised because I now understand that he was very shy. Needless to say, though, that was the highlight of our prom night.

On a more recent memory, we spend our winters at the South Padre Island Golf Club. Knowing what big KU fans we are, for Christmas in 2005, our children gave us airline tickets from south Texas to Austin, with tickets to the KU-Texas game. We flew into Austin with our KU regalia on, and me with my red and blue pom-poms. If you've been to a basketball game at Texas, you know it is like a stage production, and the fans are like a cult. I was not concerned; our boys would easily win. Well, we lost by one of the biggest margins we had in a long time, 80-55. As a proud Jayhawk, I kept my head up as we left the arena ... but I did hide my pom-poms under my coat.

CHAPTER 8

KU Isn't Just a Basketball School, You Know!

John Martin

John Martin, a 1959 graduate of the University of Kansas School of Fine Arts, is one of the country's most accomplished portrait artists. His paintings hang in more than 75 cities around the world. Martin's work has crossed many professions, including business, academia, government, medicine, and both collegiate and professional sports. He remains a passionate KU fan.

John Martin
Photo courtesy of John Martin

A good friend of mine in my office days back in the early 1960s, like me, was a KU grad. In 1964, I had a couple extra tickets to see Oklahoma play KU in Lawrence. KU had a good team with Gale Sayers in the backfield. Steve Renko, who went on to become a major-league pitcher, was the quarterback. My friend, Jim, had something else going on that day, so instead of riding to Lawrence together, he wanted to meet at the game, which was fine.

Kickoff comes along and no Jim. He hasn't shown yet. OU kicks off to KU and Sayers fields the ball on the 4-yard line and proceeds to make a brilliant runback. He was dodging defenders and making the Sooners look silly. He went 96 yards for a touchdown. The crowd was roaring after this incredible return. Just as the crowd is dying down a little, Jim and his wife show up. When I told him what they'd just missed, he couldn't believe it. He was so disgusted with himself. Throughout the rest of the game, OU pushed us all over the field. They shut us down. We couldn't get anything going offensively. They were up 14-7 with a couple minutes left in the game. The Sooners punted on 4th and 1 on our side of the field. The ball went out at the 6-yard line. Jim said, "I'm going to beat the crowd." So, he and his wife left.

Bobby Skahan, for some reason, replaced Renko at quarterback. Skahan proceeded to march the Hawks down the field. In those days, KU students took these English horns to the games. They made a really interesting noise. And, as the team continued down the field, these horns were blasting around the stadium. KU got the ball to the 15-yard line with about 9 seconds left. After a timeout, Skahan tossed a halfback pass to David Crandall. OU is all over us. Crandall got the ball back to Skahan, who dodged two tackles, avoided defenders, and made a spectacular dive over the goal line as the buzzer sounded. Touchdown! KU decided to go for the win with the two-point conversion. In one of the great calls of all time, the play went to Mike Johnson — and not Sayers — who took the ball in. We won 15-14 and the crowd went nuts. Those English horns were blasting, people were yelling and screaming. At that time, the track around the field was that red cinder dust, and as people were celebrating, that dust was flying all over. It was such an incredible, picturesque scene. Half the KU team was being carried off the field. That has to be one of the great, great scenes in KU sports history.

Another wild game I recall was the 1962 football game against Nebraska. My brother and I went to Lawrence for the game. We were about five rows up on the 10-yard line. We walked around the track to our seats. Nebraska had lost the week before to Missouri, and we could tell that they were fired up on the sideline. Sayers was a sophomore on a nice KU team that was coming along. All of the Nebraska fans were in the end zone, at the end where there used to be a cow bell just outside the end zone. Nebraska was rolling and their fans were roaring. Bill "Thunder" Thornton was the

Huskers' stud and he marched them down the field. They scored quickly and went for two. They got it and went up 8-0. Before you knew it, it was 16-0. Then, 24-0. With each touchdown, their fans were getting wild. After Nebraska went up 24-0, some of their fans came out of the stands and headed right for that cow bell. It got so bad that police on horses couldn't stop them! The game was stopped for five minutes while they tried to corral the crowd. I'd never witnessed that. There was a big fight with a bunch of guys getting hauled off. They were unruly. It was wild. Definitely more action there than on the field. Nebraska won the game, 40-16.

When you're talking about great scenes in KU sports history, one would be Wilt Chamberlain's first varsity game, which I saw in person at Allen Fieldhouse. (That was his sophomore year because freshmen weren't eligible at the time.) He set records in scoring (52 points) and rebounding (31) that game against Northwestern. Those points remain a record and the rebounds are second to 32 that Wilt got the next season. He obviously was there to show Northwestern and the country who he was. In those days, Allen Fieldhouse seated more than 17,000, and had a sunken floor, and it was packed for Chamberlain's debut. I was a student at that time. That was the first time I'd witnessed everyone in the crowd stomping their feet on the floor and making the whole place tremble and shake when we'd go on a run. I think it started then. The place was bananas when Chamberlain came. He was sensational — a man among boys. He could score and rebound, obviously, but he could press.

We were playing intramurals one time in the old gym, Robinson Gymnasium. Chamberlain dropped his books, jumped on the level of the indoor track, about 15 feet up, and did chin-ups. He was a stud athlete. He could run a 47.4

quarter-mile. He also won the high jump and was the triple jump champion in track. He was so strong. He had a move that you'd love. He'd take the ball in the key, jump up, turn around and stick out his big arm and do a finger roll. His arm was even with the rim and he'd just drop it in. He was sensational.

By luck, I was in Municipal Auditorium in Kansas City for the triple-overtime national championship game — just called the NCAA Finals — in 1957. A buddy and I were going to just go to Kansas City and watch the game somewhere because we didn't have tickets. We just wanted to be close to the action. We were passing through the old Muehlebach Hotel when a coach stopped us to see if we wanted to buy his tickets at face value. Evidently, he had an emergency in California, so he was leaving immediately. Just like that, we were headed across the street to the game. Because the tickets were from this coach, our seats were in the coaches' section, lower level. As an added perk, at half-time, they made an announcement, "Ladies and gentleman, we want to welcome the college coaches who are with us. Would you please stand up?" So we did. I loved it. Unfortunately, the game didn't turn out in KU's favor.

One that did, though, obviously, was the 1988 championship in Kansas City against Oklahoma. The first half of that game, which ended tied, 50-50, remains one of the greatest halves of basketball that I've ever seen.

I've been lucky to do several paintings for KU. One is a growing mural in the basketball office. Coach Ted Owens called me in 1979 to do a mural showing KU's All-Americas and his two Final Four teams. I had done some publication work for KU and got to know Ted. At that time, the mural was about seven feet tall and only seven or eight feet wide. It showed James Naismith, Allen Fieldhouse, Jo Jo White,

Wilt Chamberlain, Bud Stallworth, Walt Wesley and so on. I added the 1986 team to that mural when Larry (Brown) was there. Then, when they moved offices, Roy Williams wanted to do a makeover. This wall was 15-feet wide, so when Roy got to his second Final Four, I put Danny Manning against Stacey King of OU for 1988, and added the 1991, 1993, and then the 2003 Final Four teams. After the 2008 title, Bill Self called to add that, which I finished in 2009. Now it's about 20 feet long. We add to it whenever they get to the Final Four. When their new offices are complete, there will be room to expand the mural.

The other art story that comes to mind is when I did a mural in 1983 for the All-America room at the Adams Center on the KU campus. The benefactor was Harry Darby, who was senator of Kansas and took over when Clyde Reed passed away, and Darby filled out his term in Washington. Harry was instrumental in the American Royal and head of an engineering firm in Kansas City, Kansas, on Strawberry Hill. His son-in-law was Ray Evans, a two sport All-America, and one of the best athletes in KU history. Harry wanted to do a series of murals honoring the All-Americas. Ward Haylett, who was an architect and a K-State guy, for crying out loud, mentioned my name as a possibility to do the murals.

They selected me, so I went and interviewed Harry Darby, who was 91 years old. He was an amazing man. He had a barn behind his house with incredible artifacts. He knew numerous celebrities in Hollywood. Really, he was just an interesting person. When I interviewed with him, he said what he wanted done. I'd known Ray from past meetings for various projects. Mr. Darby spelled out his mission statement for this. When I left, I was on Cloud 9. I was so inspired. He had a way of doing that to a person. You'd walk on fire for him.

I started the project. The first mural was the football one. It was five feet by eight feet for 10 football All-Americas. I got to design the look of it, and we put an American flag on each mural to denote that it's All-Americas. Through the process, Ray helped me significantly with some of the colors because a lot of the photos I used were black and white. When I finished the football mural, Mr. Darby wanted to view it. The mural was so big that it wasn't easy to transport out of my office. So, Mr. Darby came over in a limo to view it. He couldn't get out of the car, so he wanted to view it from the car. Ray came to my studio on the fourth floor. He got on one end of the painting, I got on the other end and we took it down to the parking lot so we could put it in front of Mr. Darby. We carefully got it down the stairs and outside. Mr. Darby rolled down the window and said, "It looks terrific. Very good. Thank you." He rolled up the window and we took it back up the stairs. That's one of those moments that I'll never forget. We used the same process for the other murals but we found a way to deliver them to Mr. Darby at his office on Strawberry Hill. Because KU had so many All-Americas, we decided that you had to be a two-timer in basketball and track. That balanced it out.

KU was great in track and field. The KU Relays, for many years, were absolutely huge. I witnessed, in 1948, world records at the KU Relays: one by KU's Harrison Dillard in the 120-yard high hurdles, and another in shot put by Chuck Fonville from Michigan.

It's amazing to me to think about some of the KU guys I've witnessed. On the track side, there was Glenn Cunningham, Charlie Tidwell, and, of course, Wes Santee and Jim Ryun. In field, there was Al Oerter, Bill Alley, and

Ernie Shelby. Ernie was a dash man, as well, but he was the AAU champion in triple jump. He was jumping 26-plus-feet every week. Ernie was in school when I was there. He was the best-dressed guy, and a great-looking guy. He was from Los Angeles, played the guitar, sang, and was an artist. He was the best-rounded person I've ever been around. He could do no wrong.

I grew up in Ottawa, Kansas, because my dad was connected to Ottawa University, including time as the president there. So, my allegiance was to them. After going to school there for two years, I transferred to KU because Ottawa didn't have an art program. Since then I've become, obviously, a huge KU fan. Sure, there have been some disappointments, but what incredible athletes, coaches, and teams we've seen in all of the sports.

Steve Renko

Although best known as a Major League pitcher for 15 seasons, Steve Renko was one of KU's last three-sport lettermen. The Kansas City, Kansas, native lettered in football, basketball, and, of course, baseball in the 1960s. Renko currently resides in Leawood, Kansas, with his wife. He remains a passionate Jayhawk fan.

My introduction to KU athletics started when I was fairly young. It was in 1947, when I was about four years old. At that time, my dad, also named Steve, played football at KU. I remember getting on the train and going to watch the Jayhawks play Nebraska in Nebraska. The thing I remember the most is the football players coming down to Kansas City after the game and they stayed all night and slept on the floor. Then, after spending the weekend in Kansas City, they went back to school. Dad stayed in touch with them after he finished playing.

Steve Renko
Photo courtesy of Kansas Athletics Archives

Dad graduated from high school in 1937. He was going to be a doctor. In 1938, he got into an accident and severed ligaments in his left arm, above his elbow. He lost use of the last two fingers and thumb on his left hand. He worked at several jobs and didn't go back to school right away. In 1947, coach George Sauer came to him and wanted him to come back and play. He weighed 247 pounds. He lost 28 pounds to get in shape. He was back on scholarship and he graduated.

We were living in Kansas City while he was going to school, at least in 1947 and 1948. I don't remember going up there much. I do remember going up with him later, though. He could get two tickets for $1.50 each or something like that, so we'd drive up and watch a game here and there. The first time, I saw Wilt Chamberlain. He was on the back hill at the student union, selling programs. Walking up to him — man, he was huge!

Even though I had that KU influence, I never thought about where I was going to go to school. The only thing I can remember is that in high school I got a couple letters. A friend of mine who was a basketball player got a few, including Missouri. I didn't get anything from Missouri. I got one from K-State in basketball. My friend and I went to Manhattan to visit. Everybody thought I was going to KU. But I never said I was.

I signed a letter of intent to go to KU. The day after, I got a call from UCLA to play baseball. My mind was made up. I was headed to KU on a full football scholarship as a fullback/linebacker. Chuck Dobson, who was a pretty good football player in high school before hurting his back, was there, too. Freshmen couldn't play varsity sports then, so we had four football games and six basketball games as freshmen.

All the games are blurred — I don't remember many. I even look back on baseball, and games don't especially stick out except for maybe one pitch here or there or little flashbacks. I can remember parts of a football game in Colorado. I remember part of a game in Lawrence against K-State. I remember playing at Syracuse. I remember the Oklahoma game. The other is when we played Iowa State at Iowa State. I had switched from quarterback to defensive back because we had a bunch of guys hurt. Bobby Skahan was there, so he went to quarterback and I went to defensive back. I had two interceptions, eight tackles, knocked down a pass, and knocked the ball loose from a tight end. Probably my best game in my whole career. The next game was Oklahoma. On one particular play, the Sooner receiver stopped on me when I had him on the sideline. I caught my arm on him, he knocked it down and dislocated my shoulder. I was out.

At that time, there were passionate fans, just as passionate as today, but there weren't as many of them. They were loyal, though. I remember playing against TCU at Memorial Stadium and we were getting beat. We were going for everything with Gale Sayers down the middle. As we were getting close to score, I threw an interception. I got booed by 50,000 people. It wasn't a big deal to me, but it was to other people. Roy Edwards, who was a big booster, sent me a letter. Ray

Evans, the great former KU player, sent me one. They were embarrassed by the way the fans reacted. I got several other letters saying similar messages.

Again, it didn't matter. KU fans were passionate then, and they're passionate now. I'm one of them. I don't go to the games as much these days only because of the crowds. Plus it's much easier to watch them on TV. Obviously, the basketball team has continued its great success, but now the football team is very exciting to watch. I'm really happy for the players and coach Mark Mangino.

Rock Chalk!

Chuck Dobson

Chuck Dobson is quick to point out that he's "proud of his mediocre career," even though he doesn't talk much about the nine seasons he spent pitching in the major leagues for the Kansas City-Oakland A's and then the California Angels. Since retiring in 1975, Dobson has been a substance-abuse counselor, house painter, world traveler, and English teacher. Dobson grew up in the Kansas City area, where he remains today.

Growing up in Kansas City and ending up at KU, it'd be easy to assume I'm a lifelong fan of the Jayhawks. Well, not necessarily so. In fact, I was more of a Missouri fan as a kid.

Coming out of De La Salle High School, I thought I would end up playing football somewhere, possibly MU. Well, they only offered me a half-scholarship in football. KU offered me a full scholarship. Notre Dame came later, but by that time I'd already signed a letter of intent to go to KU.

As it turned out, though, KU did something unexpected that sealed the deal. I hurt my back in baseball during my senior year of high school, after signing to play football. So,

I approached KU and asked them if I could play baseball instead of football and still have my scholarship. They said sure. Three days later, room, board, tuition — everything — was sealed in a confirmation letter from the university. My scholarship was fine. After that, I couldn't go back on KU and pursue Notre Dame.

It would've been interesting to play football at KU, though. Jack Mitchell was the head coach. He was really funny. He took us to the Natural History Museum there and there was this animated bear. If you punched the bear, it would come alive and make this loud growling noise. Mitchell, like some big kid, kept pushing it and pushing it to hear that growling sound. He had the greatest time with it. I figured he couldn't be all bad if he's playing around like that. I'm sure it would've been interesting to play for him.

Even though I liked Missouri, I have no regrets about going to KU because they were really wonderful to me. Except, I was baseball teammates with Steve Renko. They kept promoting him as a three-time All-America. This was in the days before Major League Baseball held a draft. Scouts signed you to play baseball by headlines, and you got money according to the headlines. I pitched a double-header one time at Colorado. I won the first game, 7-0. Fifteen minutes later, I'm back on the mound for the second game. I pitched six innings in that seven-inning game, walked two guys, and Coach Floyd Temple took me out of the game. We were winning 5-0, he took me out, and we ended up losing the game. There's a fun story about that night, when he pulled a curfew check, but I'll get back to that in a minute.

When we got back to KU, the headlines read: "Renko injured, misses series." It was a long, two-column story. The only way you knew that I pitched a double-header was in the very fine print in the box scores. I was not mentioned in any of the story. I made up my mind at that point that I was going to sign professionally. It wasn't working out too well, being in Renko's shadow. (Keep in mind, that's not Steve's fault. That's just the way it was.) I decided at that point to sign. That was 1964. I did get selected for the Olympic team that went to Tokyo that year, which was a great experience, before signing with the Kansas City A's.

I knew of Renko because he and I faced each other quite a bit growing up. He was at Wyandotte High School (in Kansas City, Kansas) and I was at De La Salle. Oh, we have some stories. I think any time Renko and I and former Royals pitcher Steve Mingori faced each other in high school,

What do you get when you put 32 K-State cheerleaders in one room?

A full set of teeth.

it was going to be a 1-0 final. One time Renko would win, the next time I'd win, and then it was the same when we faced Mingori. We traded off that way.

Back to that series at Colorado. We were in Boulder, and a guy got all of us dates that night after the game. Out of 25 players, only three guys were in for curfew, and I think one of them had broken his leg and couldn't get out of bed! Temple went berserk. He took away all of the scholarships. I think he held true to that for the most part. He came up to me afterwards and said, "I can't, in a good heart, take your scholarship away after you pitched a double-header. You're OK."

KU had great fans back then, but not necessarily for the baseball team. It was a sub-sport at that time. We had fans but hardly anyone knew about us. It was nothing like it is now.

Of course, I remained a football fan and went often to games because we could get in with our student ID. My freshman year we had Bert Coan, John Hadl, and Curtis McClinton. That's a pretty good backfield.

Since then, I've remained a KU fan. It's really been fun to see the football team be successful in recent years. I believe we have a football team now. They're definitely exciting to watch.

Chris Browning

Chris Browning lives in Olathe, Kansas, where he works for the family business, Ms. Ashley Accessories. He married a KU grad, Lisa (Koch) Browning, in 1992. All three of their children have been to games at both Memorial Stadium and Allen Fieldhouse, and all three have the same favorite player: Jake Sharp.

During the spring of 1990 through the fall of 1991, I worked for KJHK (the student radio station in Lawrence). It was an absolute blast! Part of that time, I did stats for the football broadcasts, including the game against Missouri in 1991, when Tony Sands rushed for 396 yards on 58 carries. At the time, that was the NCAA record for yards, and is still the record for carries. Another amazing stat for that game was he had 24 carries of 7 yards or more.

Later that night, the Hawks played someone in hoops at Allen Fieldhouse. Tony came into the Phog and the place went crazy. When I saw him, I ran over and asked him to be our halftime guest, which he agreed to do. I don't know if Bob and Max talked to him at halftime of the basketball game, but the student station sure did.

Like many Jayhawk fans, one of my greatest recent memories is the 2008 national championship game in San Antonio.

I was watching the KU-North Carolina semifinal game at my house in Olathe with my lucky Jayhawk basketball. We were killing them, and my wife decided to come down and watch it with me. When she came down, we were winning 40-12. UNC slowly crept back in it. I looked at her and said, "If the lead gets to single digits, you are out of here." She stayed, though, and we won. One cool moment to me during that game happened in the first half, I think, when North Carolina's Tyler Hansbrough got the ball at one of the elbows and he went to the basket. On the way, he got fouled by four of our guys and Mario Chalmers blocked the ball to about the fifth row. It was fitting that this kid from Missouri, Hansbrough, got pummeled by KU. To see our guys elevate like that felt so good. I felt no ill will at all toward Roy Williams. It was a business decision. But I still wanted the Hawks to beat them badly that night.

Immediately after the game, I looked at my wife and raised my eyebrows. She just said, "OK, go ahead and go."

The wheels started turning. I grabbed my phone, called my friend in Ft. Scott, Kansas, and asked him if he would go to San Antonio with me if I got tickets. He said yes. I called a friend who was at the KU-UNC game and asked him to track down a UCLA or UNC fan and offer him $100 per ticket. He called me back in five minutes with two to the finals. I called a friend in Phoenix and asked if he was interested. He said if I would pick him up at the San Antonio airport, he would spring for the room. "What flight are you on?" So, in a span of 20 minutes, I had two tickets, transportation and accommodations in San Antonio. "The ball" came with us on the road trip.

"The ball," by the way, is just a mini, stuffed basketball. I got it for my first son when he was born. It has a Jayhawk embroidered on it. For some reason, though, whenever I watch a game, I find this ball and hold on to it. I have a pretty good track record when I have that ball with me. I had it during the North Carolina game. I'll admit I left it in the hotel during the Memphis game. Just the sheer presence of the ball in Texas was good enough. Plus, I didn't want to get the grief from my buddies as a guy in his late 30s carrying this stuffed ball. We'd bust it out and rub it before heading to the game. There's tradition and mojo and good luck. It's just full of magic. It brought us back in the Memphis game, I'm sure.

The cool thing about that was down at the River Walk the KU bar was Rita's. It was a zoo. I ran into my mom and dad there. I saw fraternity brothers of mine who are scattered all over the country. Buddies from Brooklyn, Phoenix, Wichita and everywhere else were there. What a blast!

That said, though, I'm more of a football fan than a basketball fan. I thought Glen Mason was a great coach and did some great things here. I get way more nervous during football games than I do basketball games. I'm a total numbers guy. Based on our winning percentage, we have a much better chance of winning each basketball game than football game. It's mathematically correct, so I don't get nervous about basketball games. In San Antonio, when we were down by nine, I looked at my friend and asked him how he felt because I felt pretty good. He did, too. The Memphis fans around me were incredibly nervous. When Chalmers hit that shot, you could see that Memphis was done. It's not always like that in football.

A lot of games have stood out. The one that felt really good is the day that we kicked the crud out of Nebraska in 2007, 76-39. Seventy-six points was having your cake and eating it, too. When I was a kid, there was a Nebraska game in Lawrence when the Cornhuskers scored at will. (There

Kerry Meier and the Jayhawks won the battle with MU at Arrowhead in 2007.
Photo courtesy of Jeff Jacobsen/Kansas Athletics

were a lot of Nebraska games in Lawrence — and many other places around the league — that went like that.) In this particular game, they kept scoring and we were going three and out. They were up 27-0 late in the first half and they had the ball again. They scored with very little time on the clock and then went for two. The score was 35-0 going into halftime. Their coach, Tom Osborne, gave some baloney answer for why they did that. But they did that year after year! So, for us to hang 76 on them was incredible. I think we could've scored more. I think Coach Mark Mangino called the dogs off.

I have a friend who went to the Nebraska game in 2005 when KU won 40-15. I told him I was taking him to each

Nebraska game after that. During the blowout of 2007, we looked at each other with disbelief. This was Nebraska!

Another game that stands out was the one against Texas late in the 2004 season when Vince Young was the quarterback for the Longhorns. They came to Lawrence ranked No. 6 in the country and we had three wins. But we were in a dogfight. We led for 58 minutes. The controversial Charles Gordon play happened right in front of me. The Texas defender jumped Gordon's route. In my opinion, the defensive back stood there and Gordon did what he did to get around the guy. That was a baloney call to make against Gordon.

That game did convince me that Mangino was the right coach. We were getting better players and we were tougher. We weren't backing down from anybody. And the week after losing the heartbreaker, the Hawks went to Columbia and blew out the Tigers, 31-14.

Speaking of Missouri, the 2008 game at Arrowhead isn't one I'll forget. How could anyone forget that! That game had every ounce of emotion for both teams. My wife and I went there for our anniversary. We got a room downtown, had a nice dinner, and then went to the game at Arrowhead. The weather was cold, but it didn't matter, especially when Todd Reesing made the game-winning play to Kerry Meier. I love listening to Bob Davis' audio call of it. You'd think his eyeballs were shooting out of his head when Meier made the catch. That was incredible. I love listening to that on YouTube.

I have so many game memories because I started going to football games with my dad in 1975. The Jayhawk stud then was Nolan Cromwell. We went to the game in Lawrence against Oklahoma when Cromwell injured his knee. That hurt our football team and killed Bud Moore's career as KU's head coach. Cromwell was a star, though.

My parents are KU grads and I've always had it in my blood. When your parents are alumni and stay involved with the school and go to games, you naturally inherit that. So, growing up, there was ZERO doubt where I was going to school. My dad joked that I could go to any school in the state as long as it wasn't in Manhattan. That wasn't going to be a problem for me. I was then — and will always remain — a Jayhawk.

Basketball, Shmasketball ... We Do More Than Play Basketball

Dan Sanders

Topeka

In 1999, my brother Dave and I attended the Kansas Sports Hall of Fame induction at Abilene. John Riggins was one of the inductees that night. I grew up in Seneca, Kansas, and played high school football against Riggins when he played for Centralia. John was like a man on the field with a bunch of boys. At the autograph table, I introduced myself to him and John indicated he remembered me. I told this story to my son Ryan, who responded, "Dad, there's no way you're going to tell me a Super Bowl MVP remembered you!" Ah, but he did, Ryan. Or at least he said he did. To have a Jayhawk legend say that is fine with me.

How many Nebraska freshmen does it take to change a light bulb?

None. That's a sophomore course.

Mark Stallard

Overland Park, Kansas

You can watch hundreds of football games on TV or from the stands, and during the tensest moments of any game, trying to guess what a coach and his players are saying to one another, let alone thinking and feeling, is almost impossible. Most head football coaches leave their emotions in the locker room while walking the sidelines, but you can usually tell their angst level from the tightness in their eyes.

I was able to get a good look at a coach's eyes on a few occasions.

For three seasons I was a student trainer for the KU football team, which means I helped tape players' ankles before practice and games, handed out towels and ice packs, administered some therapy for injuries, and played water boy during game timeouts. I also got a look at the world of college football, a view very few students — let alone fans — get to see. And I saw a lot of losing — Kansas won just six games during my tenure as a student trainer.

The best thing about my student trainer experience was Dean "Deaner" Nesmith, one of KU's grand legends of athletics, who I had the honor and pleasure of working for those three seasons. Deaner played football for the Jayhawks from 1933 to 1935, and was the head trainer for KU athletics from 1938 to 1983. His blood and Jayhawk loyalty ran as true and as blue as Don Fambrough's.

My second year on the football staff was 1977, a season that had not been kind to KU. The Jayhawks lost two close games on the road to UCLA and Miami, and were hammered by Oklahoma, Iowa State, and Nebraska in Big 8 Conference play. Going into the finale against Missouri, KU had just two wins: a 14-12 squeaker against Washington State, and a 29-21 victory over hapless K-State. The Tigers hadn't had much of a season, either, with just four wins, and a victory by either team in "The Border War" would erase a lot of the year-long frustration both schools had suffered.

The Jayhawks controlled the game from the outset and led throughout. But in the final minute of play, Kansas faced a third-and-long situation from their own 4-yard line — they held a precarious 24-20 lead. A timeout was called, and KU's head coach, Bud Moore, a strict disciple of Alabama's Bear Bryant, huddled with Brian Bethke, the Jayhawks' quarterback, to discuss the situation. When we weren't working during the games, I would walk along the sideline and watch the action on the field. During crucial situations, I just stopped, inched as close to the field as possible, and watched.

During this crucial timeout, I happened to be standing next to Deaner, who was standing next to Bud Moore. A look of perplexed anxiety covered the coach's face, but I also noticed that Bethke appeared calm and ready. He waited for his instructions, but Coach Moore wasn't talking. After an awkward silence, Deaner leaned slightly toward Moore and quietly said in his gravelly voice, "Take the safety, Coach." When Bethke took the snap moments later, he backed up quickly and then ran out of the end zone.

Kansas won the game, 24-22.

CHAPTER 9

For the Love of
the Jayhawks

Erik Ashel

Erik Ashel is a Special Projects Producer at Metro Sports, an all-sports television station in Kansas City. Erik is a graduate of KU's William Allen White School of Journalism (Class of 2000). In 2008, he produced the documentary "Border War," detailing the history of the Kansas-Missouri rivalry.

Erik Ashel
Photo courtesy of Erik Ashel

Walking down Mt. Oread is supposed to serve as the symbolic end to your journey as a student at the University of Kansas. For me, that moment didn't arrive until almost eight years after that glorious day in the spring of 2000. I was done with school, but in my mind, my time at KU wasn't finished. The walk down the hill in May was nice, but in reality, it was the sprint down Massachusetts Street in April 2008 that made my journey complete.

I don't think my decision-making process would fly with most high school guidance counselors. I was lucky, though. As it turned out, KU had a pretty good journalism program. Of course, that's not the real reason I came to Lawrence in 1996. My intention was to study basketball ... not broadcasting. That's why I'd always hoped to be a Jayhawk, and it was easily the main criteria in my college choice.

I remember that somebody once told me about the "world famous" school of journalism at the University of Missouri.

They said MU even had its own television station. It didn't matter. If I wanted to be an astronaut, Missouri could have had its own space station, and its own moon, and I still would have said "no way." As far as I was concerned, Missouri was already its own planet. Obviously, even at a young age, my priorities were solidly in place.

Fast forward a decade or so ... and I'm begging not to be sent on a free trip to a KU Final Four. Sounds crazy, right? I know. Well, it's complicated. I did end up studying something other than basketball in college. I received a journalism degree, which turned out to be nothing more than a certificate revoking nearly all of my passion as a sports fan. It's pretty much all dead to me ... NFL, MLB, NBA ... I couldn't care less. It's a job. It's a fun job that I love, but it's still work. Sports will never be the same. There is, however, one exception ... and it shines on top of that hill in northeast Kansas.

In my job I feel like I have to fight to remain a passionate KU fan. That means not getting too close. It requires buying tickets instead of using a press credential. It means requesting to not cover NCAA Tournaments and Final Fours. It also means trying to sneak in a vacation request in December for the last week in March and first week in April of the following year. Until 2008, it meant a seemingly eternal attempt to symbolically put an end to my college career by experiencing a National Championship in Lawrence.

They say you remember the losses more than the wins. I can't say I really remember every detail surrounding KU's loss to Arizona in the 1997 Sweet 16. However, the feeling in the pit of my stomach is something that will never go away. That was my freshman year. The national title was a foregone conclusion. Then, it was just ... gone.

I had endured every disappointment since 1988, but it's different when you're on campus. You crave that earth-shaking moment ... that crowning victory ... that party you'll remember for the rest of your life. Every four-year class entering KU after 1982 had seen the Jayhawks advance to at least one Final Four. A Final Four was nothing to me. I was going to see a National Championship. I was sure of it.

1998 held the same expectations, but didn't end any better (Ugh ... Rhode Island). 1999 and 2000 were two of the most disappointing seasons in the Roy Williams era. I had spent four years at KU. I graduated, but I still had never accomplished my original goal.

Of course, as soon as I moved away, KU was back in the Final Four. Atlanta was just as close to my new home in Memphis, but it didn't matter. I knew I needed to be in Lawrence for this to be official. Unfortunately, the drive back to Tennessee was almost as excruciating as the loss to Maryland.

I love the city of New Orleans, but in 2003 I made the nine-hour drive north (to Lawrence) instead of the six-hour journey south (to New Orleans). I couldn't make it back for the semifinal game. My friends told me how great it was to be downtown after the win. I was jealous, but I'd be on Mass. Street by 9 a.m. on Monday, preparing for the bigger party. Next to the loss to Arizona in 1997, nothing's been tougher to accept than 18 missed free throws and a three-point loss to Syracuse. Maturity never taught me to take these things in stride.

This story is mine, and it was also the plight of every Jayhawk. Never has a group been so blessed and, at the same time, felt so cursed. KU had more basketball tradition than anyone. It had the best fans, the best coach, the most beloved players, the most historic gym, the most dedicated town. KU had everything ... except the NCAA championships to back up its claim as the greatest place in the country to play, coach, or be a fan of college basketball.

It was always a devastating blow to a Jayhawk fan's ego. I thought I'd lose control when Florida won its second NCAA basketball title in 2007. In my short-sighted and frustrated view, a football school had taken just 12 months to accomplish what Kansas had achieved in 110 years. It might have just been the liquor talking. Regardless, it felt like the entire KU nation was about to give way under its own weight.

I've been crushed, but I've never cried after a loss. But I was on the verge of tears at the 2:12 mark of the National Championship game on April 7, 2008. I had done everything right. I'd maneuvered my way out of work, out of a trip to San Antonio, back onto Mass. Street with thousands of 21-year-olds, and sure enough, back into my typical deep, dark place.

This isn't happening, I thought. The stars were aligned ... Brandon Rush coming back, the 20th anniversary of the 1988 title, Manning in the Hall of Fame, four No. 1 seeds, beating Roy in the Final Four. There was no way that this was going to happen again. But a five-point lead melted into a nine-point deficit ... and a town ready to explode with joy quickly turned into the most depressing place on earth. Luckily, 2:12 was enough time for a miracle to save our world.

The rest of this story is also the most difficult to put into words. I could recount every play, but since this is written for Jayhawk fans, I doubt I need to. After all, this is my story, but it's also every Jayhawk's story. The names and places are interchangeable, but the cleansing emotion inspired by that shot, that overtime, and that wonderful night will stay with us forever.

For me, it meant everything. Basketball is why I fell in love with KU as a kid, and why I wanted to come to Lawrence. In turn, coming to Lawrence is how I grew up, why I have my career, and it's where I met many of my best friends. In reality, basketball was the origin of what led me to the most meaningful period of my life thus far. I guess that's why I never feel like I have to apologize for loving KU "too much" or taking wins and losses "too seriously."

> Why did Texas choose orange as their team color?
>
> You can wear it for the game on Saturday, hunting on Sunday, and picking up trash along the highways the rest of the week.

Well, I had my party, and I guess I can finally accept that trip to the Final Four next time. The wait is over, and the moment was everything I thought it would be, and so much more. It felt like a lifetime, but eight years after walking down that hill, I was sprinting down Massachusetts Street. Minutes earlier I was a 32-year-old man, out of place in a bar full of 21-year-old kids. Now, I couldn't be more at home, and I couldn't feel any younger. Just like the thousands of KU fans flooding into downtown beside me, I had finally experienced a dream ... and I felt like I had finally graduated.

Dennis Minich

Dennis Minich graduated from KU in 1988 with a bachelor's degree in liberal arts. He has worked at the University of Kansas Hospital as a Senior Media Relations Specialist since 2001.

I have a lot of great KU memories, but one of the best happened in the late 1960s. I went to a church youth retreat at Lawrence, and following a lock-in on Friday night, we all went to the KU-Colorado football game. I don't remember who won, although I am pretty sure it was KU. I walked all over Memorial Stadium and I remember the crowd, the smell of popcorn and the Jayhawks. But I knew I was going to be a Jayhawk when I saw Jim Ryun walking the sideline with his camera. I had read of his running, knew he was a Church of Christ boy, and he was studying to be a photographer. I ran and took his picture and while I didn't talk to him, I realized that at KU there were people like Jim Ryun just walking on the sidelines of the football games. That was pretty amazing to me.

When I was in school at KU, I lived a couple years in the Jayhawk Towers. I knew some of the players from around the complex but not more than to say "hey" once in while. One night my roommate and I were going out for the evening and we were discussing who was going to drive. We were going back and forth on who would drive. The elevator opened a couple floors down and basketball player Paul Mokeski got on. He said, "It's OK, guys, I'll drive." We all thought that was funny. Pretty much the rest of the year, whenever we ran across Big Mo, there would be a driving comment like "OK, where are we driving tonight and are you driving?" We were at a game one night sitting a couple rows from the end line. There were no press seats in those days so players would run into the crowd once in a while. Mokeski was down close to us and some player came flying into the seats. In the commotion, he must have noticed us sitting there because he used his hands to simulate a steering wheel and pointed at himself. It was a hoot. About five or six years later when he was playing for Detroit, I went to a Kansas City Kings game on a press pass and went in to interview him after the game. I told him we were old driving buddies and he got a good laugh out of it.

I hate MU. In 1976, both KU and MU had OK football teams and the final game of the season would determine which team would go to the Sun Bowl. It was in Lawrence and I remember the student announcer on the sideline kept the student section pumped up with, "Come on, the winner goes to the Sun Bowl, let's let them hear us." KU won, 42-24, went to the Sun Bowl and that's that. The next year, KU was pretty bad. Missouri was still mediocre and it came down to the KU-MU game for MU to qualify again for the Sun Bowl. My roommate was dating a girl from MU so we went to Columbia for the weekend. I think we were on student tickets she had borrowed. but I didn't care. I wore my crimson and blue stocking cap and scarf and walked right into the student section. The taunts were relentless and, ironically, the student announcer was firing up the crowd by taunting our team that was out of the hunt. He said, "Come on everybody, you know the winner goes to the Sun Bowl." KU laid it on MU that day. It was 41-14. It was a palindrome, but by the end of the third quarter most all of the MU students had left, so there was a couple dozen of us KU fans and we yelled, asking how to get our tickets to the Sun Bowl.

Without a doubt the greatest KU memory was following the 1984 basketball season. They made the NCAA tournament and were assigned to the first two rounds in Lincoln, Nebraska. I don't really remember how the trip came about, but I know that this was Larry Brown's first year and we loved how the program had changed. Ray Meyer was coaching DePaul for the last season and they were playing in the first game of the doubleheader. My nephew, Steve Beaumont, was a yell leader that year and so he got us tickets. The Meyer game was pretty unremarkable and KU lost to Wake Forest, so we were absolutely devastated.

But the whole story was the trip home. Driving up there, it started out a pretty much normal March day. It was gray and cold. When we got to Lincoln, it was colder and there was talk of snow, but we didn't think a whole lot about it.

During the DePaul game there were some announcements about the storm front and road problems, but based on how it was when we went in, we still didn't think much about it. I think there were actually announcements to the effect of "If you don't have a room, you'd better get one." Between games there was some chatter about the snow, but I still don't remember being overly worried about it. When we left, that all changed. It was snowing so hard it took forever to get to our cars. My oldest brother was driving and his son, our nephew, Steve, a very good friend, Jim Murray, and I headed home. My brother, Russ, decided early on there was no way we were making it home. So we stopped at the first couple motels we found and tried to get rooms, but they were full. We headed toward home and made it to Nebraska City. There was a restaurant there and we decided to stop, call around for a room, eat and spend the night. I called my boss and said I wouldn't be in the next day and others in our group made their arrangements. The wait for a table in the restaurant was going to be a couple hours because it was packed and no one was leaving. Anyone with a table was just sitting. Ironically, it was a lot of KU people and I remember most of the Kansas City media being there, including all of the TV guys. Russ talked to the restaurant folks and determined that all the rooms in town were full, so we had no choice but to slog ahead.

We went to a nearby gas station and loaded up on crackers and candy — that was dinner. Jim Murray slipped the gas attendant $20 and told him not to let Russ pay for gas. Russ pumped the gas and went in to pay. The attendant said that during snowstorms gas was free and we were good to go. It took Russ quite a while to figure that one out because he spent about an hour talking about the free gas during blizzards. But the trip home was absolutely awful. We spent most of the trip going no more than 10 or 15 miles per hour. Like typical snowstorms, there were some people who couldn't drive so there were the spinouts or people going overly slow. It took us nearly 11 hours to get home.

I just remember that day started out so fun and with such promise, but between losing and snow, it ended horribly. But we are Jayhawk fans and a little snow wasn't going to stop us. Plus, in Nebraska, you get free gas during blizzards.

Richard Young

Richard Young graduated from the University of Kansas in 2007 with a degree in Business - Marketing. He currently lives in downtown Kansas City, working as a commercial insurance agent at Garry & Associates Insurance Agency.

There Were No Tears

Through my years of being a Jayhawk fan, I had always pictured this moment in my head. Although the players in my daydream changed with the current roster, the image never did. Watching the clock wind down as our players and fans erupted in a jubilation rarely felt, certainly not in my lifetime. Hearing the booming voice of the crowd count down, 3 ... 2 ... 1 ... into a thunderous crescendo of cheering as tears would build in my eyes. It was vivid enough to think it may be real for a second, until I shook the dream out, realizing that it was once again a fantasy, and I would have to wait another year. Then there was 2008. Then there was Mario.

I had given up. I always had faith in this team through-out this season, especially throughout this game, but it was over. Down 9 with 2:12 to play ... no team could come back from that; especially us. The roller coaster of emotion in being a Jayhawk fan the last 20 years told me it was impossible. The Bucknells and Bradleys, the Acie Laws and Hakim Warricks sucked my hope from this game. The lead started to shrink, yet the only thought in my head was "The closer the game becomes, the worse this loss is going to feel." Deep down, I knew we were going to lose in the most devastatingly dramatic fashion possible. I couldn't watch. I thought convincing myself of the imminent reality would ease the pain of the last 132 seconds.

Why do the K-State cheerleaders wear bibs?

To keep the tobacco juice off their uniforms.

Then, Darrell Arthur hits a jumper that Billy Packer called "the worst shot in basketball." I still was a desolate mess. It had happened countless times before, and it would happen again. But then, something funny happened. Sherron Collins came out of nowhere, stole the ball while toeing the line... then, with two less-than-perfect passes inside, it was kicked out to Sherron again. I knew he was going to hit the shot and skyrocket my misery into a stratosphere I had yet to see.

I began to believe. Watching the last minutes of this game was eerily similar to 2003. Missed free throw after missed free throw. Chance after chance to tie the game. When Sherron lost the ball near the basket with 45 seconds to play, instead of once again diving head first into my pool of despair, I told myself we still had a shot. More missed free throws. Then came the defining moment of my life as a Jayhawk fan. A moment I will never forget. There was some-thing so imperfectly perfect about that last play. From

Sherron pausing as he took the inbounds pass and everyone in Jayhawk Nation yelling "Go, Go!!!" Then the trip and eventual dump-off to Mario. But there was nothing imperfect about Mario's shot. As I watched the ball in the air, I couldn't feel my body, but I was acutely aware that my reaction to come in the next .5 seconds would be at one of two ends of my emotional spectrum. Unbridled joy or unbelievable pain.

Unbridled joy! When I look back 20 years from now on this game, I will remember this moment. I will remember every person I hugged. I will remember the surreal feeling of thinking we actually beat the hand that fate dealt us. Overtime was a formality. From the tip, there was a different look in the eyes of the coaches, players, and fans. Everyone could taste it; it was ours. As I watched Sherron dribble out the clock with a smile on his face that only a national champion could have, I realized my daydream was becoming a reality. My daydream wasn't a daydream at all. It was real.

Something was missing. I jumped up and down. I hugged and high-fived every person in sight. Everything was happening like I had always imagined, except for one thing: tears. Perhaps the anti-climactic nature of overtime is why. Perhaps I just misjudged what my emotions would be. I was somewhat disappointed.

My eyes opened at 3 a.m. for no apparent reason on a random Wednesday night a few weeks later. I couldn't fall back asleep. My thoughts reminded me of the looming workday, but I couldn't fall back asleep. Then, as if someone was sending a subliminal message, Mario popped into my head. I immediately got up, walked to the living room, and turned on my DVR to watch the last minute of regulation. I watched Sherron drive up the court, and Mario hit the shot. Then ...

tears. Three weeks after the game, I had finally cried. I started to dry up, and then Jim Nantz yelled out "Rock, Chalk Championship!" and I lost it again. There was a sense of relief. A sense of finality. It had truly sunk in. We are National Champions.

Nikki Blaylock

Nikki Blaylock lives in Kansas City, Missouri, where she was born and raised. She has a Bachelor of Science degree in Housing and Interior Design, and has worked as an interior designer for two years. She grew up playing volleyball and basketball, which made watching KU basketball more fun.

My dad is the reason I'm such a die-hard KU fan today. When I say die-hard, I mean that I will most likely tear up after a close loss as if I were a player on the court after his last game. I don't remember how old I was when I experienced Allen Fieldhouse for the first time. It was a night game in the middle of the week. I just remember being in grade school and sleeping in a warm car on the way back to Kansas City. As I got older, I had fun getting KU T-shirts and posters before the games. A memorable moment was in 2003 when my dad, my brother, and I went to greet the team at Allen after they made the Final Four. The team was supposed to arrive about 1 a.m., but didn't get there until three hours later. The Fieldhouse was about one-third full but it sounded like a regular game when the team stepped foot onto the court. The greatest feeling I ever had at Allen was during the MU game in 2009. It was so loud I could feel the building vibrate through my body.

Being such a die-hard KU fan was especially difficult on me because, well, I live in Missouri. So, most of my classmates and friends were MU fans! I can't count how many times I've been asked, "Why do you even like KU? You live in Missouri!" Many of my friends can't understand it. They obviously don't understand what it means to be a Kansas Jayhawk regardless of where one lives. The toughest time I ever had with a Missouri fan was my first two years of college. I attended Missouri State, in Springfield. My roommate was from a small town outside Columbia. She was as big of an MU fan as I am a KU fan. Our dorm room was divided with MU gear on her side and KU gear on mine. The worst was a stuffed MU Tiger that sang the school's fight song any time you pushed its paw. The first time MU and KU played each other during my freshman year, she would squeeze the Tiger's paw whenever MU would make a basket. She did this for about the first five minutes of the game. Unfortunately, the tiger disappeared before the next game. Somehow the tiger ended up under some dirty clothes in my laundry basket. I may have had something to do with that. Even though I haven't seen her in four years, she still manages to send me messages and "talk trash" on those rare occasions when MU beats KU. Even though our teams were rivals, we were very good friends.

When I was younger, summertime always seemed to be the best time of the year. Now working in my career field, summer vacation no longer exists. Basketball season has become my favorite time of the year. If it weren't for Kansas basketball, this definitely would not be the case. Watching KU basketball together has been a tradition in my family since I was in grade school. When I was growing up, my mom would watch part of a basketball game with my dad, my brother, and me, but did not often sit down to watch the entire game like the rest of us would. That has changed dramatically since 2007. Now, my mom makes me so nervous when we watch a game together sometimes I have to leave and go watch by myself in another room.

My younger brother and I both played basketball from first grade all the way through our senior years in high school. Over those years my mom learned about the game. In the beginning, when we were kids, she just wanted everyone to have fun and wasn't too concerned about winning. Winning became more important to her when I got to high school, but I don't think she fully understood how my dad, my brother, and I felt after a KU loss. She wouldn't want them to lose because it would mean she would have to deal with a house full of grumpy people the rest of the day, and possibly the next few days.

It had always been my brother's dream to go to school at KU. That dream started when he was a ball boy for the basketball team as an eight-year-old. That dream came true in 2005 when he started his freshman year. That's probably when my mom became more interested in KU basketball. She learned the names of all of the players and could recognize them on TV. Today, instead of doing something else and keeping an eye on the game, she will sit down for the whole game. That is great except she has a hard time controlling her excitement. She is now much more vocal and animated than she used to be. She reminds me of a little kid playing a video game that moves around with the controller, just as their character does on the TV screen. After a key basket she will jump out of her chair and yell, "YES!" I understand that reaction because all of my family — including me — will do that. However, my mom has taken this to another level. Since I am an athlete, I have learned how to stay composed during close games. She, on the other hand, does not seem to understand how to do this. She cannot sit still during the close games. She jumps at a time when I am not expecting it and her reaction causes me to flinch. During late-game free throws, she starts to react before the shot is even taken. By this time she has moved from her chair to the ottoman directly in front of the TV. The ball hasn't even left the shooter's hand when one of Mom's legs comes off the floor and both arms are raised up over her head with one of them usually covering her eyes! I am constantly telling her, "Mom, chill out!" She made the National Championship game against Memphis almost impossible for me to watch, although I was probably just as excited as she was. The last minute of the game I had to sit directly in front of the TV on the floor so I couldn't see her, because she was making me so nervous!

I don't think she will ever go back to the way she was when I was younger. Back then, when we went to a game at Allen Fieldhouse, she would just wear either a blue or a red shirt. Now when we go to a game she's decked out in one of her many KU shirts like the rest of my family, even with a Jayhawk tattoo on her cheek. Now, a KU loss hurts her just as much as it does my dad, my brother, and me. She will even talk trash with her MU friends, which she never did before.

I love my mom and it's been great to be able to share this with her. I just wish she could tone it down a little during the games, before she gives herself or me a heart attack.

Charles Gruber

Lawrence

Many years ago, my fandom was at its manic height. When the rare occasion occurred that we lost a game, my kids would ask my wife, "Mom, is Dad going to be OK?" My wife would frequently ask me, "How much time until tipoff?" This led to my establishing the Grubertron2000 Tipoff Countdown Timer. I still have it going on my website.

These days I've mellowed a bit. My wife no longer has to hide the sharp knives if we lose. My friends who are therapists no longer feel compelled to call and offer counseling if we miss foul shots at the end of a game. On the flip side, winning the National Championship *never* gets old.

Tish Merritt

KU Class of 2003

I was a student at KU from 1999-2003. Not once in the four-and-a-half years I attended KU did I ever get on the floor of Allen Fieldhouse. (I'm an aspiring actress, so of course I'd want to stand up in front of the whole Fieldhouse. Attention-monger, I know). As soon as I graduated I received a job with KU Endowment, which came with perks. If there were no donors available for basketball games, those in the office could get down on their hands and knees, promise their first born, paint their noses brown, and hope and pray for tickets.

One time I was the lucky brown-noser. I scored some awesomely close seats that night. I was seriously beaming ear to ear, so when a hypnotist (performing at the Fieldhouse for the evening) asked for volunteers, without thinking, I raised my hand. That night I plucked around like a chicken, acted like Jennifer Lopez and did other embarrassing things ... all in the name of love. There's just something about Allen Fieldhouse. You feel something incredible once you walk through the doors. Heck, it may be magic in the air. Whatever it was still has me proud and beaming to this day that I performed the chicken dance in front of a packed house.

I love Kansas basketball!

Rock Chalk Jayhawk!

Chris Reaves

KU Class of 1992

I don't personally have any superstitions, but there is a big group of us — anywhere from 15 to 40 or so — that get together for every single KU basketball and football game at an Overland Park bar called Maloney's. We've been doing it for several years. There are people in the group who have some crazy superstitions about what time they get there, what they wear, where they sit, etc. But probably the best superstition is one that started and now has a Pavlovian effect on us.

What would happen is that the very second every KU game would end, the manager of the bar would automatically turn down the TV sound and crank up the bar's music system. Of course, it's mainly to keep people from leaving and to get people energized, etc. Well the system they used would ALWAYS automatically begin with a song called "Without Me" by Eminem. (It starts with the lyrics, "Two trailer park girls...") Of course, KU wins about 80-90 percent of the time, so the song became kind of a default victory song for all of us in the bar. It became so automatic that sometimes you can hear people chanting, "two trailer park girls" instead of "Rock Chalk" toward the end of games.

Well, about a year or two ago, Maloney's got rid of that system and installed one that would "randomize" the song selection. So, that Eminem song wasn't the default anymore. Our group got so used to hearing and associating that song with a KU victory — think Pavlov's dog and the bell — that now the manager of the bar will ALWAYS hang out at the jukebox during the last few minutes of every game and put money in to specifically choose and play that Eminem song for us (victories only, of course). The best part about it is that the manager is a die-hard K-State fan and HATES doing that.

Photo courtesy of Jeff Jacobsen/Kansas Athletics

Authors

 **Matt Fulks** writer, editor and broadcaster, started his journalism career while attending Lipscomb University in Nashville, Tennessee. He is the author/co-author of 14 books, including *CBS Sports Presents: Stories from the Final Four* and *Echoes of Kansas Basketball.* He also is a regular contributor to various publications, including kcmetrosports.com — the website for Kansas City's all-sports TV station Metro Sports.

 **Rich Wolfe**'s books have sold well over a million copies in the United States. Wolfe has authored the best-selling books in the history of Notre Dame and the Chicago Cubs. The Iowa native is the only person to appear on both *Jeopardy!* and ESPN's *Two-Minute Drill.* In 2006, he was inducted as one of Leahy's Lads at Notre Dame.